LinkedIn

For

Veterans

Debra Faris

LinkedIn for Veterans
Published by
Solutions Press
Newport Beach, California

© 2019 Debra Faris
ISBN: 978-0-9996497-6-3
All rights reserved

This is a work of non-fiction. The ideas presented are those of the author alone. All references to possible results to be gained from the techniques discussed in this book relate to specific past examples and are not necessarily representative of any future results specific individuals may achieve. Information presented is correct to the best knowledge of the author at the time of publication.

The author of this book has no connection of any kind whatsoever with LinkedIn Corporation or any of its subsidiaries or allied companies. LinkedIn Corporation has given no endorsement of the strategies outlined in this book, implied or explicit.

Business Strategy:
A Salute to Veterans Event

Host Debra Faris & Co-Host Eric Holly

"Helping to change the city of Inglewood one brick at a time."

Erick Holly

Planning Commissioner City of Inglewood
President of the Inglewood Chamber
President NAACP Inglewood & South Bay

This man will change the world starting with Inglewood. I met Commissioner Holly as a coincidence. I shared with Melissa that I wanted Police & Fire Departments represented at the event because they hire Veterans, whose character traits include military skills dedicated to service, discipline and leadership. Melissa said, "You have to talk to Erick at Inglewood Chamber." I later found out Erick is also a Planning Commissioner for Inglewood.

The 9/11 tragedy is a day we in America will never forget. The Inglewood Chamber of Commerce held a Police & Fire appreciation luncheon Sept 19 to honor the service of police officers and firefighters who risk their lives to save people. These unsung heroes are not recognized on a daily basis but every day they put their lives on the line to protect and serve our country.

Erick's vision is to help local business. "Our mom and pop businesses are the heart of every community," he says. "Without a doubt our current residents need to feel comfortable with the major developments occurring in the city, so we keep them in the conversation, so they understand what's going on with the changes."

www.LinkedInToVeterans.com

iii

Contents

Business Strategy: A Salute to Veterans Event iii

Introduction ix

Acknowledgements xi

Chapter 1 What's my Purpose... on LinkedIn? 1

My Influencers: Floyd "Shad" Meshad 1

Why LinkedIn? 3

Online and Offline - EHarmony 7

Authenticity and Transparency 8

Shifting Your Mindset 8

Who Am I? I am...! 10

I am Big Bird 12

Chapter 2 Get Started with Your Story 21

My Influencers: Floyd "Shad" Meshad 21

Your Story: Use your imagination like JK Rowling 22

A Picture is worth a Thousand Words :) 24

Character is Everything 27

Formatting: Start with the end in mind 27

SEO: What is it and how does it help you? 29

Chapter 3 Click, Click, and Connect 39

My Influencers: Greg Raths 39

Connections 40

Trust Your Intuition 42

Making Connections Anywhere 44

Who should I invite? 44

Pieces to the Puzzle: Memory Jogger 45

Should I accept anyone? 47

Chapter 4 To Engage or Not to Engage 55

My Influencers: Albenago "Al" Arseo 55

Who Viewed You? 56

Shared Connections Are Gold 58

To Endorse or Not to Endorse 60

Positioning and Aligning 62
Chapter 5 Networking to the Next Level 67
My Influencers: Joe Molina 67
Your Million Dollar Message 68
F.O.R.M. 71
Qualify like a CEO 72
Networking Tips. 73
What is Left-Brain Right-Brain connecting? 74
Go Deep in Your Connections 77
Network Like Your Life Depends on It 77
Relationship Currency 78
How to Win Friends and Influence People 79
Chapter 6 Groups, Tribes, and Communities 85
My Influencers: Stacy Sanchez 85
Seven Ways to Pick a Group 87
What's a tribe? 91
Group Etiquette & Settings 92
Groups are like the Super Bowl 50 93
Diversify Your Groups. 94
Chapter 7 Follow-Up and Follow-Through 101
My Influencers: Tom Muzila 101
Follow-up is a Winners Game 103
Reach Out and Touch Someone. 105
Ask, Ask, Ask for Help and Referrals 105
Who are your Top Five Companies? 106
Identify your Top 20 Connections 108
President Reagan wrote Five Thank You notes a day .. 109
Chapter 8 Recommendations, Marketing 117
My Influencers: Isaac Belden 117
Market like an Icon 119
Credibility through Celebrity 120
People Also Viewed 124
Who knows Who. 126
Keep in Touch Marketing 126

Who did they recommend & who recommended them? 127

Testimonials are your best friend 128

Be a producer using iPhone Videos 129

Chapter 9 Jobs, Industries, and Culture 135

My Influencers: Jesse Medina 135

You are more than your resume...............................137

The Difference Between Recruiters, Headhunters & Outplacements...138

Top 12 Big Connectors - Recruiters & HR.................138

Websites are Your Research Tool............................141

Positions vs. Industries...142

Think International 144

Organizational chart: Who connects to who?............148

People Don't Hire Resumes, They Hire People...........148

Working for Non-Profits 150

Find Connections in Your Top Five Companies 150

Yes, Barbie® has turned 57 153

Chapter 10 The Power of Charity and Volunteering 159

My Influencers: Larry Thornton..............................159

Attitude of Gratitude 160

You Have a Calling..162

Random Acts of Kindness.......................................163

Pay it forward. "Making a Difference".....................168

Together we are more..169

Chapter 11 Entrepreneurship & Mentors 177

My Influencers: Jeff Hoffman..................................177

Questions are the Answer 178

What is ROI vs. ROT 180

Strategize your Success...181

Billion Dollar Mindset..182

Who's Your Wingman?..184

Social Trailblazers...185

Chapter 12 Reinventing Yourself & Beyond 193

My Influencers: Janet Chin 193
Coaches, Mentors & Role Models 195
How the Internet Changed Opportunities 197
Visions & Visualizations... 198
Looking Outside the Box 201
Think Tank & Mastermind....................................... 202
Amazing Grace, a Pondering Thought...................... 203
Chapter 13 Veteran Advocates 209
My Influencers: Chris Naugle 209

Author Index

Robert Adamik	Chapter 9
Al Batinga	Chapter 2
Mark Brenner	Chapter 2
Rodney Brown	Chapter 10
R. Michael Buhehler	Chapter 13
Jeffrey Duff	Chapter 13
Thomas Evans	Chapter 5
Dom Fausette	Chapter 6
Megan Fenyoe	Chapter 1
Eldonna Lewis Fernandez	Chapter 7
Kurt Glasgow	Chapter 3
Dan Godwin	Chapter 1
Lisa Lockwood	Chapter 8
Ryan Matthews	Chapter 6
Chris Megison	Chapter 10
Mark Schultz	Chapter 13
John Shin	Chapter 13
Steven Spriggs	Chapter 4
Robert Stohr	Chapter 12
Gregory Taylor	Chapter 11
Dr. Benjamin Zvenia	Chapter 9

Introduction

In today's world, where things are so easily, instantly obtainable on the Internet, it's necessary to bring back old-world traditional relationship-building. *Veterans in LinkedIn* was crafted to teach veterans, executives and entrepreneurs the necessary skills to build long-term relationships with the right people through networking, engagement, and follow-up.

In addition, this book will teach them the entrepreneurial and leadership skills necessary to develop "an eye for opportunity." They will develop their underlying intuitive skills, which are the basis of all human connections, enabling them to build productive, long-term relationships that will shape their destiny.

Veterans in LinkedIn is for veterans, executives, entrepreneurs who want to help each other leverage LinkedIn for what's next in their business opportunities in a rapidly changing world. Social media has gone from being social to your sharpest tool for business adventures. LinkedIn can help you find new clients and connect with like-minded people to network with and build relationship currency.

LinkedIn has more than 500 million members and is more than a rolodex. This unique book shows you 12 strategies from how to leverage the one million groups to finding the perfect charity to make a difference. Check out the incredible stories and how they are using LinkedIn.

Acknowledgements

Thank you to all the people who were instrumental
in helping create this book:

This being my 4th LinkedIn book, *LinkedIn for Veterans* was a must
honoring my son Dan Godwin, who started his career in ROTC and
continued with the Air Force. I realized how those on LinkedIn can
serve those who served us. My first book *LinkedIn for College
Students* was dedicated to my son Phil Godwin, who wanted to be
an anthropologist. Thank you for your love & your spirit that will
forever be a part of me and thank you Phil's girls, Scarlet & Sophie
and his wife Denise. I'm so blessed to have you be his love to light
up our hearts. Gina, my daughter, I never knew someone could be
as smart as they are beautiful, and her boys August and Preston
who take after their mommy in every way.
They keep me
appreciating the little things.

Thank you, all the people who have influenced
and contributed to my life.

Lee Pound, you are the whole enchilada; a brilliant writer,
grammatical king, patience of a saint, work ethics of a Thomas
Edison, support like a whole squad of Dallas Cowboys
cheerleaders.

George Carson, who stepped in as the best Boy Scout to help redo a
website that needed a Superman. George, your family deserves a
special thanks for the time you spent to help this "Veteran mission
to Make a Difference."

Chapter 1
What's my Purpose...
on LinkedIn?

Soldiers, when committed to a task, can't compromise. It's unrelenting devotion to the standards of duty and courage, absolute loyalty to others, not letting the task go until it's been done.
--John Keegan

Floyd "Shad" Meshad

PTSD Pioneer, President & Founder NVF
Lifeline for Veterans
888-777-4443
Crisis, Suicide & Information

My Influencers: Floyd "Shad" Meshad

Because I knew my project for veterans would be one of the most important things I've done, I knew I needed to identify the people who had really made a difference, the ones who were in the trenches working for veterans. There were many to choose from. I asked my friend Jeff Duff, CEO of Airstreams Renewables, Inc., an organization that provides job training and employment opportunities for vets transitioning out of the military. He didn't hesitate. "The person who has done the most to improve the lives of vets is Shad Meshad. He's been doing that for over forty years. You have to meet him and talk to him."

Jeff told me that Shad had been a psychiatric officer in Vietnam. Coming home, he made his way to LA and started working in the streets with alienated Vietnam Vets. He'd founded and directed the Vietnam Veterans Re-Socialization Unit at the VA Hospital in Los Angeles, and he was among the first to study what became known as Post-Traumatic Stress Disorder, or PTSD. Later he was instrumental in PTSD being recognized as a diagnosis in the DSM (the Diagnostic and Statistical Manual of the American Psychiatric Association). He'd been called to Washington during the Carter Administration to replicate his model of treatment for Vietnam Veterans, which led to his co-authoring legislation that created the Vet Centers for the VA, now in over 300 locations across the country. A traumatologist, he was called to New York to treat first responders after 9/11. He'd been on *60 Minutes* and *Nightline* and countless radio broadcasts. Meshad served on the faculty of the International Critical Incident Foundation, on the Board of Directors of the Green Cross Project, and as President and Board Member of the Association of Traumatic Stress Specialists. A published author, he blogged for the *Huffington Post* for six years on veterans' issues. **In short, there was nobody with Shad's history and depth of experience.**

Jeff made the introduction. When I called Shad at the National Veterans Foundation, he said, "Come on over!" This was LA. I was four miles away. I went immediately. Walking into the office was like stepping into a museum or a shrine. Every wall of the conference room where we met was covered with photos illustrating the history of the NVF, begun in 1985 as the Vietnam Veterans Aid Foundation, later renamed the National Veterans Foundation to reflect its inclusion of veterans, male and female, of all wars. After our conversation, Shad showed me his office, where I saw, among others, commendations from President Carter. I felt like I was standing in the presence of history.

The National Veterans Foundation, a non-profit foundation, is now in its 34th year. It's served over 450,000 veterans and their families. It's program for women vets is growing. The impetus for the

NVF was Shad's determination that vets be able to talk to other vets to get answers they needed quickly: information they needed about how to transition from the military, how to reconcile the invisible wounds of war, how to access their benefits and navigate the complicated bureaucracy of the VA. Today, the NVF's Lifeline for Vets crisis and information hotline receives over 12,000 calls per year, and that number is rising with these two longest-running wars in our nation's history. Shad's model of vet-to-vet communication is the gold standard. His ability to handle crisis and suicide intervention calls is legendary.

Why LinkedIn?

Facebook, Twitter, Google+, Instagram, LinkedIn, Pinterest, Tumblr, Flickr, Meetup; the list goes on and on. Social media sites are cropping up left and right on the internet and are here to stay. People interact and connect on social media sites, forming virtual communities and networks, sharing information and ideas. With all these choices, why use LinkedIn?

You may think social media is only for people chatting endlessly about personal details, gossip, or sharing recipes and photos. What difference can it make for you? Isn't social media is for young people? The answer is simple. LinkedIn is about building relationships and deep connections. In business, you built relationships both online and offline with your fellow co-workers, professional associates, recruiters, even competitors. You can deepen these relationships by connecting with them on LinkedIn. Then you expand your connections and relationships using LinkedIn. You build a team of connections and relationships that will help you in the future as you search for a new opportunity.

Although relationships and connections are important in general, they are far more critical for those who find themselves in transition. The best way to find a job is through connections, both who you know and who knows you. When you build a team of individuals who know you, like you, and want to help you; you make finding the right job far easier. LinkedIn is the perfect place to start. When you build your business profile, you are building your future business persona. People begin to learn what you're all about.

Singleness of purpose is one of the chief essentials for success in life, no matter what may be one's aim.
--John D. Rockefeller, Jr.

Start now! In today's competitive job market, you cannot afford to be left behind. All professionals, including veterans, need to use and become experts at LinkedIn, the sooner the better. Building profiles that represent who you are, show your authenticity and character, and showcase your talents and awards will give the business world a glimpse of what to expect as they review your profile.

You have a track record of experiences and successes that you need to share, so the world knows who you are and what you can do. LinkedIn is your tool for spreading that message. Its members' names appear at the top of Google search rankings because it has more than 500,000,000 members, massive traffic, and constant change in content. It even outranks websites people have paid tens of thousands of dollars to create. This gives you a big advantage when potential employers or customers search for you. In addition, LinkedIn's wide range of privacy options allows you to control what others see about you.

I call LinkedIn your mini-website because it gives you many of the same benefits as having your own website. You can connect and build relationships, get your needs shared, and showcase your skills and talents.

LinkedIn offers many avenues to create and discover your ideal job or future clients. That's why I suggest you build your profile in three parts.

1. First, complete the basics and develop a "complete" profile on LinkedIn.

2. Second, design your profile so that busy executives and top recruiters can read it easily.
3. Third, show your personality and your connection with the real world in a way that gives you high credibility and attracts the right people to you.

Even though LinkedIn is designed as a way for business owners, veterans, executives, and professionals to connect, do business, and find jobs, it is still social media. Many people think it is enough to put up their profiles, which are all about themselves, and expect to attract the people they want without interacting. This is the wrong approach. To get from point A to point B with potential connections, you must communicate with them. Business is all about talking with people, creating connections, and building communities. To succeed on LinkedIn, you must create engagement and partake in or even create your own community.

500 Million Members in 200 Countries

Article   Talk   Read   Ec

WIKIPEDIA
The Free Encyclopedia

Main page
Contents
Featured content
Current events
Random article
Donate to Wikipedia
Wikipedia store

Interaction

Help

LinkedIn

From Wikipedia, the free encyclopedia

LinkedIn (/lɪŋktˈɪn/) is a business and employment-oriented service that operates via websites and mobile apps. Founded on December 28, 2002,[4] and launched on May 5, 2003,[5] it is mainly used for professional networking, including employers posting jobs and job seekers posting their CVs. As of 2015, most of the company's revenue came from selling access to information about its members to recruiters and sales professionals.[6] As of April 2017, LinkedIn had 500 million members in 200 countries, out of

When a client of mine says, "I thought this wasn't social media," I say, "That's what I thought in the beginning, too. Then I found out

I was wrong and became very excited about the opportunities the site offered."

When you see these opportunities, you will think, "Oh My Gosh, Gold, Gold, Gold, Gold!" LinkedIn is the most phenomenal site I have ever seen. That's because you get tons of free publicity with your LinkedIn profile.

Once you get started, you will build an edge over your competition for the best positions now available or soon to emerge. But you must approach it as you would any other serious professional representation of your business persona. This book will take you through all the steps.

When I chased after money, I never had enough. When I got my life on purpose and focused on giving of myself and everything that arrived into my life, then I was prosperous.
--Wayne Dyer

Whether or not you have already decided to jump into LinkedIn, this book will show you how to get it done right and make your best professional impression. LinkedIn is a unique channel that gives the consumer multiple dimensions and tons of value, all for free. It has no hosting fee and no monthly membership fee (although members can pay for an upgrade account which gives extra benefits).

Be sure to ask yourself these questions. What is your intention on LinkedIn? Is it to find a job or connect with known associates? Is it to find groups that can help you market your products or services? Is your network going to be online or offline or both? Identify the people you want to meet and the message you want to send. Then connect, follow up and be part of the communities that keep you connected.

LinkedIn is recognized for their influencers. We have added a few of our own.

Online and Offline - EHarmony

The most successful online, offline internet communication vehicles are in the infamous dating world led by companies like EHarmony and Match.com, which allow their members to seek relationships that fit their criteria, ranging from friendships to dating to meeting someone with whom they can spend their rest of their life. LinkedIn works in a similar fashion except it is centered in the business world. You connect with other members, build relationships, and use those relationships in your career.

Each time you look at LinkedIn and its members, you will find people that interest you and people you want to connect with. Maybe someone shared how they accomplished goals in a specific position, or maybe the groups they joined might interest or benefit you.

These are all ways to connect with other human beings. You can also see employment histories, where people started and how their careers advanced through the years from, for example, a copy clerk to Senior VP of the Western Region for a billion-dollar company. As you continue to search and explore, you see life and careers from a different perspective.

You can incorporate your offline connections in LinkedIn as well. Connect with your family, other veterans, friends, and business colleagues as you build your network. Since you already have a relationship with these offline connections who are like you, start with them. Then as you continue to work, add the connections you make during these events to your profile. That will build your online connections and build your bucket. Expand your profile as you expand your life. Don't underestimate any connection. Sometimes one odd connection can lead to a great job. Use LinkedIn to foster both your online connections and your offline connections. Build your networks and develop relationships that help you accomplish what you desire.

Authenticity and Transparency

Building an authentic profile on LinkedIn requires skill and evaluation. To show people who you really are, you need to dig into your character traits, values, and skill sets and make sure that the image you're painting for viewers represents you. The more authentic you make your profile; the more value your connections will have to you. You only get one chance to make a first impression. Be true to yourself and allow your readers to get a feel for who you are.

At a Tony Robbins seminar many years ago, the three most important things I learned were to know your purpose, know your intention, and that questions are the answer. I got off track many times, slowed down, collected myself, and started to ask better questions, which led to better results. Nobody can change your results for you. You are the only one who can change your life and you do it by asking, "What results did I get and how could I do it differently to get better results?"

We will receive not what we idly wish for but what we justly earn. Our rewards will always be in exact proportion to our service.
--Earl Nightingale

Einstein said, "If you keep doing the same thing over and over, you will keep getting the same result. That's called insanity!" This is why questions are the key to a powerful LinkedIn profile.

You may ask, "What if my job experience isn't that exciting?" You are more than just your job experience, so, in a following section, I want you to ask, "Who Am I?" which will begin your journey on your new path.

Shifting Your Mindset

It is important to know your mission and purpose for connecting on LinkedIn before you start. If you start with the end in mind, setting up your profile and making important connections will create a more effective message.

Know why you're on LinkedIn and what you want to accomplish before you start, and your outcome will be aligned with your goal.

Mindsets are beliefs about yourself and your most basic qualities. Think about your intelligence, your personality and your talents. Are these qualities fixed traits that can never be changed or are these traits that you can change and cultivate throughout your life?

There are two basic types of mindsets, fixed mindset and growth mindset. A person with a fixed mindset believes that their basic traits are fixed qualities that they cannot change. With a growth mindset people believe that their most basic abilities can be developed through dedication and hard work.

So, you ask, how does this relate to LinkedIn? The mindset that you approach LinkedIn with will dictate your results. Just like life, if you approach LinkedIn without understanding all its dimensions and details and don't use its flexibility, you will wind up with results different than you expected. Those who think they can set up a pretty profile and that people and jobs will flock to them automatically are sure to be disappointed.

When you approach LinkedIn, remember it is a mindset connecting with others and building relationships. Mike Ferry™ teaches a course called *Mindset, Skills, Action, and Motivation* that shows people how all these components work together for success. You start with the right mindset and the rest falls into place. If you approach LinkedIn with the mindset and strategy of knowing where you want to go, who you need to meet, and ask the right questions as you build your profile, you will find LinkedIn to be a valuable tool in your networking.

I once shared a story about my skydiving adventure with a CFO (chief financial officer). He said, "Who would jump out of a perfectly good airplane?" That was his mindset. He wanted to keep his feet on the ground.

I said, "I understand why you might feel that way. But I did it, you didn't. Wouldn't you like to know what I learned from it?"

Even if you never plan to jump out of an airplane, you can still benefit from the knowledge I gained and how I felt. Everyone has their own mindset. Sometimes it benefits you to take on someone else's mindset or at least share their experience, so you can learn from it.

When I finished, my friend/client said he didn't realize he was looking through such a narrow perspective and that he would have missed possibilities for collaboration. He is a left-brain expert, analytical and detailed, where I have a creative, exploratory, communicative, curious side; therefore, when we collaborate, we bring added value, whether in a company or a relationship.

Who Am I? I am...!

Who am I? Have you ever sat in your room on a quiet Sunday afternoon and pondered that question? You know your name and what city you came from and what you look like. But when you really get right down to it...Who am I? And once I figure out who I am, how do I tell everyone else?

Early in their careers, many people are quick to pick a field and jump in without thinking about their passions and without taking time to outline their desires and visions.

When this happens, a progression of jobs creates a career and before we know it we are in our early fifties, burned out, unhappy with what we're doing, and living unfulfilled lives.

To succeed, you must learn the truth of who you are. The famous Greek philosopher, Socrates, said, "Know Thyself." This is one of the deepest truths in life. You must know who you are before you can achieve a happy, fulfilled life.

People don't understand the significance of the many bits and pieces that make up their lives. They think one job was a waste of time or didn't benefit them or that a boss was too harsh. Later in life they realize that everything they ever did made them the people they are today.

For instance, early training in honor, trust and integrity followed you as you moved into responsible positions such as Manager, Director, CEO or CFO. Past opportunities create benefits for an individual's future, because in the end it's all about your character.

Man masters nature not by force but by understanding.
--Jacob Bronowski

You need to portray your character in your LinkedIn profile; because if you do it correctly you will send a powerful message to the people you want to connect with. Identify key character traits that describe you and incorporate them into your profile. The more your profile reflects your genuine self in an authentic and transparent way, the more chances you have of connecting with the audience you desire. You need to find keywords that identify who you are, what you like, and what you want. You will recognize these words when they resonate with you. If you think about the word for more than five seconds, it belongs in your profile. Keywords that resonate with you and describe who you are create an in-depth LinkedIn profile that will attract the people you want to connect with as you continue in your professional career.

The next questions you need ask are: What are the goals of your connections? What are your goals for the communication you will have with people on LinkedIn? What are the goals of the communities you are part of?

Make a very clear statement that says, "Here's who I am and here's who my clients are." If you are in finance, write down all those characteristics, print out profiles of about 100 other financial people, and highlight all the things that resonate for you.

When you ask yourself these questions, you begin to think about the message the people reading your profile are receiving. What does your profile communicate about you and how will your audience interpret that message? If your message isn't clear to you, it won't be clear to them. Put yourself in their position; think like your recruiter. Does your profile show off your talents, strengths, and accomplishments? If not, fix it! This is your opportunity to brag about yourself. If you're not confident doing that (a lot of us aren't), have a friend read your profile and ask for their input. Listen as they brag about you; include their words in your profile. You're amazing and everyone deserves to know about you!

People may hear your words, but they feel your attitude.
--John Maxwell

Ensure that you read your profile once you have completed it and that it conveys the correct message in the correct tone. You want to attract people to you and increase your chance to build relationships. If your profile is poorly worded or unattractive, it may cost you the jobs, orders, business, relationships, or closeness that you want. You only get one chance to make a first impression. Make your profile shine and shout out your greatness.

I am Big Bird

I love documentaries. One night as I was scrolling through Amazon, I saw *I am Big Bird* and thought it was a little kid's movie, but it turned out to be the real-life story of Jim Henson and Caroll Spinney, who was one of the original puppeteers on the Muppets on Sesame street. We often miss the biggest part of LinkedIn, which is that if we don't know who we are, how are others supposed to like us, know us and trust us.

Know thyself.
--Socrates/Plato

This extraordinary movie is about how the writers wrote a part for Big Bird but the part they wrote didn't fit the human actor Caroll

Spinney's personality. They tried and tried but the actor and part refused to work. Spinney told his lifelong friend to pick someone else who could do the part. Jim refused to let him quit.

Then he gave Spinney the script and dressed him up as Big Bird and suddenly the part worked. Spinney went on to turn that role in a 30-year career, an amazing piece in history.

Here are This Chapter's Business Consultant Influencers

As you read these profiles, look for possible referrals for your needs.

Is there something in their story you connect with?

Could you gain a new idea or insight for your business or career?

Who do you know or who do they know that can help both of you?

If you needed help or wanted to buy a product, what would it be?

How do you follow up when you meet someone?

When people view your profile, how do you want them to feel?

Do your tribes line up so you could be Power Partners?

What are your favorite questions to ask in an introductory call?

Daniel Godwin

Program Manager
United States Air Force

During High School I was introduced to the ROTC program. Six years later after graduating from LMU I was an officer. Starting out Minot AFB, ND and Assigned as a Missile Maintenance Officer on the LGM-30G Minuteman III ICBM System.

Today, I'm an Section Chief, Global Positioning Systems (GPS) Requirements Assigned as an Acquisition Program Manager. In addition I am in the Reserves as the Individual Mobilization Augmentee, Space Based InfaRed System (Space Based Missile Warning System).

SPECIALTIES:

▶ Led maintenance section of 48 Airmen, responsible for the preventative and corrective maintenance of electronic, security, communication, and power subsystems; located at 150 Launch Facilities and 15 Missile Alert

▶ Directed processing, early-orbit operations, and on-orbit sustainment of eight weather satellites valued at $2.1B.

▶ Led government/contractor team comprised of 56 personnel; responsible for the integration, test, and launch planning of two satellites and launch vehicles valued at $1B.

▶ Managed cost, schedule, and performance of spacecraft integration & test contract valued at $593M; oversaw execution of service life extension programs worth $99M

▶ Led team of 160 personnel from 12 organizations; responsible for launch and early orbit test planning, execution, & operational transfer.

▶ Managed cost, schedule, and performance of spacecraft integration & test contract valued at $615M; responsible for oversight and execution of $60M annual budget.

► Led two maintenance sections, comprised of 45 Airmen, responsible for the preventative and corrective maintenance of 170 nuclear command and control communication systems valued at $638 M; located at 150 Launch Facilities and 15 Missile Alert Facilities across 8,500 sq miles.

► Acted as chief assistant to the maintenance group commander; primary liaison between executive office and two squadrons, comprised of 470+ personnel.

1. **What movie touched you by its meaning or inspired you?** Apollo 13, 1. It is about space 2. Problem solving solutions with limited resources

2. **Who in your childhood was a major influence that helped shape your life?** Mom, loyalty to my brother and sister, plus perseverance and tenacity to get thru tough situations

3. **Who now is a Mentor, Coach or Strategist that is on your advisory council?** The GPF chef engineer he is very intelligent with great vision and innovation

4. **If you could be anyone for a day, who would it be and what experience can you envision?** Truman... World war 2 experiencing decision making, as it entering the war and understanding why he chose what he did

5. **What discipline could someone learn from you?** Project management

6. **If you could have any superpower (or be any superhero), what/who would it be and why?** Dr strange, he can do magic and time travel

7. **When "winning someone over" do you think facts or emotions carry the day?** Emotion. People who are Charismatic and have passion it moves people to action

8. **If there were one problem in the world you could solve, what would it be?** Poverty

Daniel "Dan" Godwin, PMP United States Air Force
https://www.linkedin.com/in/danielgodwin1/
♜ daniel.f.godwin@gmail.com ☎ 949-533-6218

Megan Fenyoe

LCSW Veteran Best Selling Author
Public Speaker and Trainer
Podcast Host
Founder of the I Am Enough Movement

I have been an LCSW since 2008 and I am licensed in both Michigan and California. I worked for 12 years in the child welfare system and in 2012, I accepted a medical commission as a Captain in the Air Force. I provided intense Mental Health and Substance Abuse treatment to Active Duty members, Veterans and their families

I separated from service in 2014 and began working full time as a Substance Abuse Therapist in a hospital. After working in the hospital setting for a few years I made the decision to leave the corporate world and in 2017 I began my own Private Mental Health Practice alongside of my Mindset Coaching business.

In my private practice, I work with individuals, families and adolescents in the areas of substance abuse, trauma, anxiety, depression, self-esteem, communication and relational distress. My passion is helping people live life full of passion, strength and meaning.

I'm trained in CPT (Cognitive Processing Therapy for Trauma) and Seeking Safety for substance abuse/trauma as well as other treatment modalities. I provide tele-health or face to face sessions.

Everyone has a unique story. Therapy is a safe place to come and deeply explore that story. We all get stuck from time to time in patterns of unhealthy thinking, behaving, and relating, and sometimes we need help changing those patterns. Therapy works in such a way that you gain insight into areas of your life and leave feeling empowered.

I offer support, validation, empathy, and a safe and respectful place to share dreams, hopes, fears, and triumphs. I help clients accurately assess their challenges and identify ways they can change, capitalizing on the strengths they already have and encouraging them to build new ones.

Megan Fenyoe

linkedin.com/in/meganfenyoe

Websites

- meganfenyoe.com/speaking/(Book Me as a Speaker)
- meganfenyoe.com (Company Website)
- calendly.com/meganfenyoe/20min (Book Free Strategy Session)

Email

megan@meganfenyoe.com

Twitter

- missionstrongSD

The Soldier's Life

The soldier's life is not for all
A soldier must be willing to give his all
He is overworked and underpaid
A truer patriot was never made
Ready to go at any time
Wherever there is trouble or the first sign
His courage and honor are unsurpassed
Ready and willing to complete the task
Travelling to lands both near and far
He stands his post and looks at the stars
Wondering what he might have done
If he had not chosen to carry a gun
Remember the next time that you are driving by
And see the flag flying proud and high
That somewhere out there a soldier stands
Weary and cold in a foreign land
Protecting our country from our foes
Standing tall and proud come rain or snow.

Author: SSgt. Scott E Hilligoss

Chapter 2
Get Started with Your Story

For those of us who had to fight for it, life has a flavor that the protected don't often comprehend.
--Bob Wieland

Bob Wieland

Iconic Inspirational Speaker
Vietnam War Army Veteran
Double Amputee

My Influencers: Floyd "Shad" Meshad

Bob Wieland was named the Most Courageous Veteran in America and is known as an Iconic Inspirational speaker. As a Vietnam War Army Veteran, Weiland lost his legs to a mortar mine in 1969. After recovering from his injuries, he was inspired to become a marathon participant. Over his lifetime he has finished many marathons, often taking multiple days to finish. He is the only double amputee to finish the difficult Kona, Hawaii Ironman race without a wheelchair. He "ran" across America with 4,000,000 steps on his hands, taking three years, eight months, and six days to travel from coast to coast.

When his squad walked into a minefield, a member of his unit stepped on a booby-trapped mortar, Wieland rushed to give first aid but he, too, stepped on an 82mm buried mortar, a round designed to destroy tanks.

He speaks at conventions, corporate meetings, military bases, universities, high schools and churches.

A former four-time record holder in the bench press, his best lift of 507 pounds was disqualified for not wearing shoes. Bob commented saying, "How can I wear shoes, I have no feet," and laughed. The next day Bob found over 100 messages asking him to be a guest speaker at colleges and conventions in his mailbox.

One great example is ten times more powerful than great advice.
--Bob Wieland

Your Story: Use your imagination like JK Rowling

"Imagination is more important than knowledge, for knowledge is limited to all we now know and understand, while imagination embraces the entire world, all there ever will be to know and understand," Albert Einstein said.

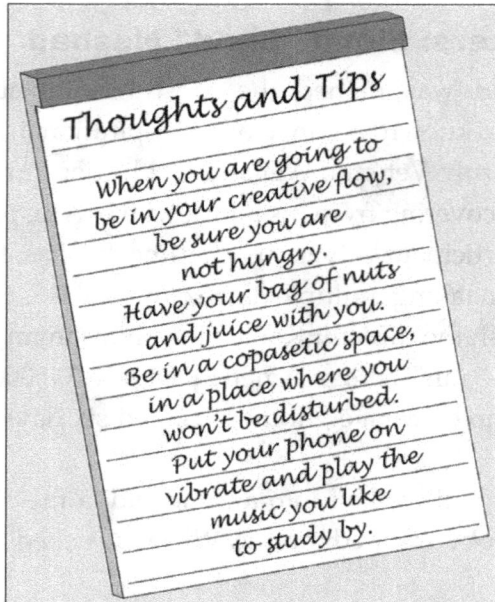

> ### Thoughts and Tips
>
> When you are going to
> be in your creative flow,
> be sure you are
> not hungry.
> Have your bag of nuts
> and juice with you.
> Be in a copasetic space,
> in a place where you
> won't be disturbed.
> Put your phone on
> vibrate and play the
> music you like
> to study by.

When it comes to your resume or your LinkedIn profile, you want to write like J.K. Rowling. *Harry Potter*, Rowling's most famous work, was all imagination. Use your imagination like she did.

Rowling gave us the idea of calling a regular human a "Muggle" and wrote the novels from the perspective of wizards. Look at your resume on LinkedIn from the perspective of the wizards (your recruiters and connections). You don't want to be viewed as an ordinary "Muggle" but want to be chosen to receive on your 11th birthday, like Harry, the letter accepting you into Hogwarts School of Witchcraft and Wizardry. Lily's sister Petunia lived an ordinary lifestyle, but Lily did not. Lily was accepted into Hogwarts while Petunia was not. Portray yourself as the person recruiters are looking for. Use words in your resume that draw recruiters to you.

Rowling created the amazing wizard Dumbledore, who could see through to who a person truly is. Dumbledore knew when he was just a student at Hogwarts that Tom Riddle was evil to his core. Many years later Tom became Voldemort. Dumbledore could read your LinkedIn Profile and see straight through to the real you. He could tell if your description is just pieces of your resume hashed into the LinkedIn Profile.

Not everyone is like Dumbledore. You must show who you truly are in your description of yourself. Your connections will not read between-the-lines because they are not Dumbledore. Present yourself as if you were trying to get Snape to see who you really are, not the pretentious person he considers you to be because he knows who your father is. Who you choose to be will convince the Sorting Hat to place you in Gryffindor and not in Slytherin.

Appearances can be deceiving, but they do matter. No one thought Neville Longbottom would become a hero. He appeared to be the dorky outcast who was never good at spells. In the end, Neville Longbottom stood up against Voldemort when everyone thought Harry was dead. Over time, we learned that the actor who portrayed Neville was a very handsome young man.

This story shows that appearances can be deceiving. In the beginning no one expected much from Neville, but he surprised everyone when he turned the Boggart from Snape into Snape in his grandmother's clothes. Don't let your appearance make people believe in you less. Let your picture show who you are and what you can do. Appearances are everything, just as Snape was terrifying to Neville but became a person to laugh at in his grandmother's clothes. You can change the way others perceive you by changing your profile picture on LinkedIn.

Think of your connections as your wand. The wand chooses the wizard, according to Ollivander. Your connections choose you, but they don't do everything for you. The wand doesn't make the magic but is a channel for the magical spells to be made.

Your connections are the same. Whether you choose your connections, or they choose you, you need to master your connections to produce the result you want. That result is like severing a connection with the Avada Kadavra spell or lighting your way with a Lumos spell. If you don't use your connections, they will do nothing for you. If you learn to master the craft of connecting with people, they will carve a path for you in the darkness like a Lumos spell does.

A Picture is worth a Thousand Words :)

This phrase is widely attributed to Frederick R. Barnard, who published an article, *One Look is Worth a Thousand Words*, in *Printer's Ink* in December 1921 on the effectiveness of graphics in advertising. He attributed the phrase to "a famous Japanese philosopher" although he later admitted he made up that origin and that he hired a calligrapher to put it into Chinese characters in the 1920s (see image below).

Even given this somewhat sordid history, the phrase does point out an important truth. The first forms of written language developed from a series of pictographs, first the ancient Egyptian hieroglyphics, then the cuneiform script of the ancient Sumerians. The ancient sailing merchants, the Phoenicians, then created the first known alphabet from these pictographic scripts.

Even before alphabets, ancient cave dwellers used images to convey important information with drawings of floods or men hunting mammoths on cave walls. Use of images has always been deeply entrenched in the human experience.

As time passed, the importance of the image to civilization has not changed and will never change. We as humans use our sight to make decisions about what to wear, what we will eat, where we will sleep, and who we will be attracted to.

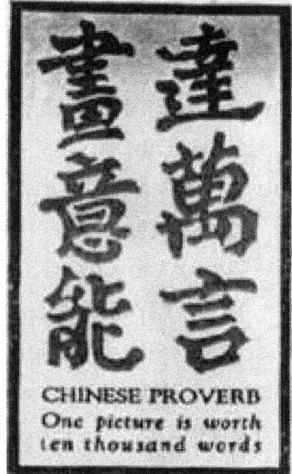

CHINESE PROVERB
One picture is worth ten thousand words

The images you use on LinkedIn are important. If you have no picture, people may think less of you. If your picture is unprofessional, it might turn them off. A visitor will look at your picture and decide in 10 seconds if they want to know more about you. In those first 10 seconds, you must make your great impression that invites people to check you out.

Lori Hart   1st
"Lori Hart About Face" Celebrity Make-Up Artist & Anti Aging Authority, Creating Timeless Beauty in You!
Greater Los Angeles Area | Health, Wellness and Fitness

Current   Lori Hart About Face

Send a message   Endorse   ▼   500+
                                                        connections

In networking and business, as a veteran you need to play the part. If you play golf with a business partner or meet a new client at the driving range, you don't wear a suit and tie, even if you are a finance industry professional who wears a suit and tie to the bank every day. On the golf course, you would wear a polo shirt and

Bermuda shorts or a golf t-shirt and a pair of khakis. You wouldn't wear a suit to play on a Saturday night, but you would wear a suit to meet the HR Manager when applying for a job.

Many times, you only have one instant to make a good impression on LinkedIn (and in life). How do you do that? You need a picture that fits as seamlessly into your profile as a window frame melds into a million-dollar house. Your picture shows who you are in your industry. When your picture doesn't fit expectations, you give your viewers a sometimes-unconscious sense of unease.

Not all people use a simple head shot. I've seen people in full baseball gear in their profile pictures to show they are a coach. Remember that this is only good in moderation. Too much creativity can give mixed signals to your viewers.

Success comes from taking the initiative and following up... persisting... eloquently expressing the depth of your love. What simple action could you take today to produce a new momentum toward success in your life?
--Tony Robbins

Always keep your photo as clean and simple as possible. The background in some pictures can be distracting. It is better to pose outside by a tree than use a fake generic background like a pretend beach with a beach ball, because truth creates the vibrations that attract people to us. Use a background that best represents your industry but is not too busy.

You don't have to use a traditional studio and pay a lot of money to get a good portrait. Today's smart phones have high resolution cameras and make it easy to upload a profile picture in just seconds.

A great photo will include: a hairstyle that shows your face; clean, pressed, and appropriate clothes that fit the part; and a smile, one that appears as if you are looking at them though the camera lens.

The best advice I can give you is to look at hundreds of pictures on LinkedIn in the industry that you are considering.

When you upload a new picture, LinkedIn will share it with your connections. If you have several photos you like, switch them out every so often. You never know who might see your new photo and whether it might be the trigger that gets them to refer you to the person who is looking for someone just like you in your industry!

Character is Everything

Things aren't always how they appear There are 3 million hoarders in the United States. You would never know most of them had this problem if you them at a party or worked with them in an office. Our trajectories can lead us in different paths and we never know how many ways we can help someone.

Brian Scudamore built a $150 million empire with his company 800 Got Junk, starting with only $700 because he wanted to help these people clean up their lives. Knowing your character traits helping others with their self-worth or business are ways to find your niche.

A am fascinated by how organizers and a company called 800 Got Junk transformed people's lives by helping them create new spaces and lifestyle choices.

Throughout this book, at the end of each chapter I will share my mentors and their characteristics. Below is a list of some character traits. Find five or six that express who you are. As you progress through the book, find other mentors and explore their traits. When it comes to great qualities in other people, as John Demartini says, "You can't see something in others that you don't see in yourself."

As we said in the "Who am I" section, you can use these character traits to reflect your skills in the specialties section and in your summary. Remember, some of these can be used again as your SEO keywords. Thread some of your character traits in your skills section.

Formatting: Start with the end in mind

The formatting in the Summary section is critical. You must create easy-to-read snippets that even a busy CFO will read. If the eye can't see the full picture, the visitor to your profile will flip to the next profile. Many things have changed with LinkedIn just like life evolves every day. In the beginning LinkedIn wanted people to put contact info in a designated section, but now it is common pract74ice to put your name and information at the top of the summary. I like to make sure it is in this more prominent position at the top of the summary.

Key Character Traits

Accountable	Adaptable	Adventurous
Alert	Ambitious	Appropriate
Assertive	Astute	Attentive
Authentic	Aware	Bravery
Calm	Candid	Capable
Certain	Charismatic	Clear
Collaborative	Committed	Communicator
Compassion	Comradeship	Connected
Conscious	Considerate	Consistent
Contributes	Cooperative	Courageous
Creative	Curious	Dedicated
Determined	Diplomatic	Directive
Disciplined	Dynamic	Easygoing
Effective	Efficient	Empathetic
Empowers	Energetic	Enthusiastic
Ethical	Excited	Expressive
Facilitates	Fairness	Faithful
Fearless	Flexible	Friendly
Generative	Generosity	Gratitude
Happy	Hard Working	Honest
Honorable	Humorous	Imaginative
Immaculate	Independent	Initiates
Innovative	Inquiring	Integrates
Integrity	Intelligent	Intentional
Interested	Intimate	Joyful
Knowledgeable	Leading	Listener

Lively	Logical	Loving
Loyal	Manages Time Well	Networker
Nurturing	Open-Minded	Optimism
Organized	Patient	Peaceful
Planner	Playful	Poised
Polite	Powerful	Practical
Presents Self Well	Proactive	Problem Solver
Productive	Punctual	Reliable
Resourceful	Responsible	Self-confident
Self-generating	Self-reliant	Sense of Humor
Sensual	Serves Others	Sincere
Skillful	Spiritual	Spontaneous
Stable	Strong	Successful
Supportive	Tactful	Trusting
Trustworthy	Truthful	Versatile
Vibrant	Warm	Willing
Wise	Zealous	

SEO: What is it and how does it help you?

LinkedIn is your own personal mini-website. It gives you the opportunity to advertise yourself and connect with many people. To use it most effectively, you must pay attention to Search Engine Optimization.

Use your headline (or tagline) as your advertisement. This is a powerful key to getting recruiters, human relations representatives, and positive connections interested in you. The words in your headline are a billboard with keywords that attract people to you.

Keywords are gold. They are the words you want to be known by and known for. When you get clear on whom you are your words provide clarity about the job or position you are seeking. For maximum impact, use keywords that people are searching for.

John Chow is one of the top bloggers in the world. People don't look for him by name; they just want to find a blogger. It doesn't matter how many hits you get; it doesn't matter how many connections you have.

LinkedIn Heading & Summary

Photo

Your Name
Header
Current Position
Previous Position

{SEO Keywords}
{Search Engine Optimization}

Summary Section:
Name & aka...
Slogan or Tagline
Email Address & Phone#
Website Address

Two blank rows

Your history
(no more than 5 lines)

Two blank rows

Today I am...
three lines

Two blank rows

Problem

One blank row

Action

One blank row

Results

Two blank rows

Your specialties,
two lines

It only matters what SEO words you use, because that is how the people you want to attract will find you. John Chow put every blog and writing word that you could think of in his header, his profile description, and his past experiences because that's how people will search for him.

Also use the current meaning of old words. For instance, content is the new word for writing, so recruiters looking for writers may search for content as well. You can also use other similar words such as writing, writer, and editor because some people might not search for content, but they might search for writing. In another field, instead of using market plans, I could use the word "launches." The goal is to hit some keywords people might embed in longer search phrases. If your simple keyword or two brings your profile up when a longer phrase is typed in, you will succeed in getting found.

To keep the attention of your connections, reword your header from time to time. When you edit your header, even just by a few words, the change shows up on the timeline of all your connections. That keeps you visible at the top of the search pages.

For keywords and SEO, find the words your future competitors use for their industry. As you work on your social media, spend 15 minutes to look at the profiles of these potential competitors. In each of the seven sections, the Heading, Summary, People also Viewed, Skills and Endorsements, Recommendations, Groups, and Companies They Follow, you will find the keywords they use. Note and use these words as you create your LinkedIn profile.

Here are This Chapter's Business Consultant Influencers

As you read these profiles, look for possible referrals for your needs.

Is there something in their story you connect with?

Could you gain a new idea or insight for your business or career?

Who do you know or who do they know that can help both of you?

If you needed help or wanted to buy a product, what would it be?

How do you follow up when you meet someone?

When people view your profile, how do you want them to feel?

Do your tribes line up so you could be Power Partners?

What are your favorite questions to ask in an introductory call?

Mark Brenner

Brenner Career Management, Inc.

What counts is not necessarily the size of the dog in the fight—it's the size of the fight in the dog." President Dwight D. Eisenhower

It's been over 4 decades since I returned from Vietnam. After a 15-hour flight from Vietnam to McCord Air Force Base I remember seeing protesters holding signs that threw rocks at the cab that took us to the Seattle Airport, so I could, after 362 days, finally go home. It was not until 2012 that someone casually said to me, "Thank you for your Service!" I'm not sure how I responded, but I do know that I was shocked that someone, anyone would recognize my contribution (no matter how insignificant).

After spending 40 years as a Coach & Business Owner in the HR & Staffing Industry, I sold my business to start a 2nd career. Today I work with Vets to get them the help that I never received when I returned from active duty. During the first 3 years we worked with over 500 vets which led to 350 of them getting positions.

Our Nonprofit (501 (c) (3)) Corporation is dedicated to Coaching, Assisting & Preparing all current and former Service members (and their families) with the secrets of the employment process to find a civilian career.

The coaching successes of VCX segued to the founding Brenner Career Management, Inc. (www.bcm.la) (BCM) to work with individuals, executive and businesses in the private sector & we are now conducting Career Coaching, Executive Coaching and Business Coaching for individuals and companies throughout the country.

SPECIALTIES: Executive Coach & Trainer, Coaching, Assisting & Preparing Veterans to find a position that matches their passion & skills, One-On-One Coaching, HR & Staffing Expert, Private Sector Individual

Career, Executive & Business Coaching, Individual Career, Executive & Business Coaching for Vets

1. **What movie touched you by its meaning or inspired you?** The Godfather, as violent as the picture was it was a sense of family.

2. **Who in your childhood was a major influence that helped shape your life?**
President John Kennedy,

3. **What will you do differently this year from last year or what do you want more of?**
I'm in the process of developing my coaching program so it not only meets the needs of Veterans but the needs of everybody.

4. **If you could be anyone for a day, who would it be and what experience can you envision?**
I would be Jack Nicklaus winning the Masters in 1986.

5. **What subject or argument most stirs your emotions, why?** The polarization of the political system and how it's destroying everything that America stands for.

6. **In helping others, is it better to teach them, give them, or show them?**
It's better to teach them while showing them what you're teaching.

7. **What discipline could someone learn from you?** To understand what it takes to find what you're looking for in a carrier & learn how to navigate the hiring process to find a career that matches your passion.
Mark Brenner, aka "The HR & Staffing Executive & Business Coach"

"Helping Vets & Their Families Xchange a Military Uniform for a Civilian Career"
▶818-724-9022 for Vets ▶ 818-987-7782 for the Private Sector
8580 ▶ mark@vcxchange.org for Vets ▶ mark@bcm.la for the Private Sector ▶ vcxchange.org ▶ www.bcm.la

Al Batinga

Educator, Trainer, Coach

"The illiterate of the 21st century will not be those who cannot read and write, but those who cannot learn, unlearn, and relearn. Alvin Toffler, Futurist

Teaching Business Systems & Business Planning for Business Owners & Entrepreneurs

Training Solutions For Next Level Business Owners

Coming from Guam, raised in Hawaii, I lived in a boarding house with multiple families. My humble beginning from 4 years old was scrubbing bathrooms helping my family make ends meet. By 10, we were knocking on doors, selling pots and pans to vacuum cleaners. At 19, I was part of the "The Few, The Proud, The Marines" which was my entre to World-Class training. I re-enlisted to become part of the Drill Instructor cadre: Elite Trainers.

Power of knowledge landed me with consulting and training projects for Fortune 500 s Ingram Micro, Drake International, NovaQuest InfoSystems, Kawasaki, and Hyundai

High-security TRUST

Today, my strength is assisting startups to governmental agencies collaborate at the highest levels to maximize and ensure growth in by utilizing people, hardware, and software at the highest level.

1. Who in your childhood was a major influence that helped shape your life? Drill Instructor Sgt. Abrams changed my life. He challenged me to return to the Drill Field after boot camp. He accomplished this in less than 20 seconds and a dozen words and he had no idea what those few words of encouragement meant to a very troubled kid.

2. What will you do differently this year from last year or what do you want more of? For the last year, I've been working in a field that I have no experience in - banking. I'm creating and crafting training programs with the help of many SMEs. It's fantastic living in the zone, where things are new, challenging and uncomfortable.

3. Who now is a Mentor, Coach or Strategist that is on your advisory council? I've met with Dr. Bob once a week for several years. We've developed a friendship and a common focus - helping others succeed. He has a PHD, incredible business knowledge and experience, lived through incredibly painful experiences and the most generous person I know. I am better after every connection.

4. If you could be anyone for a day, who would it be and what experience can you envision? I would unequivocally be the me that I should and could be. I've done it about 5 times in my life where I was "all out." Doing everything possible to be the best in my own spectrum. I can't imagine wanting to be anything but me in the zone.

5. If you could have any superpower (or be any superhero), what/who would it be and why? I would be the ENCOURAGER. Imagine when you are encouraged vs. discouraged. What are the differences? Night and day. Encouragement is water in the dessert, sunshine on a freezing day and a hand up to a fallen veteran.

6. If there were one problem in the world you could solve, what would it be? Discouragement: More ills in the world happen because of discouragement and hopelessness. I was a wisp away from it costing my life. Discouragement is the bane of society.

►Helped build the largest training center of its kind as the GM/President from a 15-employee operation to almost 200 employees, the flagship for now over 300+ locations worldwide.

►Worked with a billion-dollar IT company to create their training platform.

►Worked with federal government projects from the FDA to achieve President Obama's mandate of service to the public.

►Delivered tangible solutions results in a unique identity service delivery methodology for agile cloud computing.

Al Batinga, Educator, Trainer, and Coach

aka "Creating Systems & Training For Stealth Leaders & Collaborative Teams"

Microsoft SharePoint / Matrix Management / Remote Management / Collaboration

Connections

As the word connection echoes,

It travels through the universe
in vibration it hopes to touch

One Human,

One Life,

One Living Thing,

That in its Connection

It will Experience

That it too exists

Debra Faris

Chapter 3
Click, Click, and Connect

Marine Corps integrity is doing the thing which is right
when no one is looking.
--Colonel Lampart USMC

Greg Raths

Mayor, City of Mission Viejo
Orange County Veterans Advisory Board

My Influencers: Greg Raths

As people say, I am Ms. Connector. Connection is always about who you know but even more important who your connections know. So it was no surprise that my friend Simone, who lives in Mission Viejo, knew some very important people.

I asked her, "Who do you know who is a Veteran?"

She said, "Greg Raths. He was a Colonel for 30 years and is the Mayor."

The next day I was so excited I talked to my friend Richard Denzer, who is an Architect on large commercial projects. "I asked the mayor to come speak."

He said, "Greg Raths."

I said, "How did you know?"

"I was at a Town Hall meeting yesterday and heard Greg speak."

I feel so lucky.

Colonel Greg Raths is currently Mayor of Mission Viejo. He was in the United States Marine Corps for 30 years as a highly decorated fighter pilot of Operation Desert Storm, F/A-18 Hornet Fighter Squadron Commanding Officer aboard the USS Abraham Lincoln. Greg Raths also served as the Chief of Staff for the White House Military Office.

Currently serving as Vice Chairman, Orange County Veterans Advisory Council and on CA State Assemblyman Bill Brough's Veterans Advisory Committee and is running to represent the 45th Congressional District.

Colonel Raths holds multiple degrees including a master's degree from the National Defense University.

Colonel Raths came to Mission Viejo in 1978 as a young First Lieutenant, where he was assigned to the 3rd Marine Aircraft Wing at the Marine Corps Air Station in El Toro. He and his wife Luci have three children and six grandchildren.

Greg is a member of many community organizations including President of the Mission Viejo Rotary Club, Charter member of the Chamber of Commerce, Elks Lodge 2444, VFW Post 6024, American Legion Post 291, On the Board of OSO Valley Greenbelt HOA, St. Kilian's Knights of Columbus Council 6332, Association of Naval Aviation, Marine Corps Aviation Association, and UniteOC Toastmasters.

Connections

Connection… Connection… Connection… Everywhere we go, we see reference to "connections"; from billboards to TV commercials. It's perhaps one of the top ten most commonly used words. It is a buzzword across different media, but trail blazers have been spreading seeds of its inspiration, back to Roman times.

LinkedIn is multidimensional. It enables veterans to deeply explore who people are, what they've accomplished, and what they care about. As my friend Bob Donnell, says: "You are more than your business card."

While the first step is to click to connect, true connections involve patterns regarding with whom they are connected, their interests, groups, who they follow and by whom they are endorsed. A new connection for you, opens a potential kaleidoscope of connections.

I am a book lover, or more precisely, a lover of great authors. While recently perusing my library shelves, I became aware of how many authors had influenced other authors, most of whom, had also influenced me.

One title, a twenty-year old international bestseller "You Were Born Rich" was a book in which I had immersed myself, mainly because it's author, Bob Proctor, had studied from greats like Wallace D. Wattles (*The Science of Getting Rich*) and Napoleon Hill (*Think and Grow Rich*). Hill's landmark classic was first published in 1937 but remains a best seller with over 10 million copies sold.

Which by the way is a 78-year-old book that is still one of the top best sellers along with JK Rowling. If you read *Harry Potter* and haven't read *Think and Grow Rich,* you'll discover a different kind of magic.

When Bob Proctor is introduced, you hear a litany of accolades... international speaker, New York Times Best Seller, 6 million followers. But who is Bob Proctor? I discovered that he is truly a unique member of 'Humankind.' I met Bob Proctor at his mastermind event in Las Vegas, 20 years ago. The total number of people in the event were probably less than one hundred. I don't remember everyone who was there, but what was very cool or coincidental, was that at least ten participants were in the 2006 film *The Secret.*

Give whatever you are doing and whoever you are with the gift of your attention.
--Jim Rohn

The interesting part is I didn't even realize through the years, how many of them I connected with on LinkedIn. It was a real eye-opener for me, to suddenly be cognizant of how many connections I had that had languished through inattention. It was a big lesson for me.

Reflect for yourself, just a moment. How frequently in your life did you meet someone, got busy and didn't dive deeper or stay in touch? Take a real look at the people you connect with on LinkedIn and ask yourself, should I slow down, and examine what I really have enough here? If there truly are no coincidences, that each of your connections is there for a reason. Are you leveraging them?

Consider adding him to your influencer list.

Trust Your Intuition

Everything that happens in life happens for a reason. Every person you meet is a person you were supposed to meet. Some of those people will become close relationships, others you will introduce to someone you know, and others you will forge business relationships with. All of them, everyone you meet, know, and meet, can become part of your LinkedIn network. Use your intuition and be creative when searching for connections. Some connections will jump right out. Others you will have to work to find.

When I chased after money, I never had enough. When I got my life on purpose and focused on giving of myself and everything that arrived into my life, then I was prosperous.
--Wayne Dyer

Connecting on LinkedIn is like going to a networking event and collecting business cards. When you approach a stranger, you need to connect with them before they will give you their card. I forget the psychology behind this, but usually you meet somebody, you look in your partner's right eye, which is the eye on your left. This intuitive reaction helps build rapport with the person you have just met. If you don't connect, you won't get the card and you won't get anywhere when you follow up to talk to them later. It's about the relationship, finding a connection between the two of you. This is where your Sixth Sense needs to be sharp. What do you have in common with the person you want to connect with? My connection with Deepak was creativity. Look at the person or their profile and read between the lines. Did you come from the same state? Do you have similar hobbies? Using your intuition, find the piece of them that will best connect with a piece of you.

Once connected, you need to develop relationships with people. Relationships need to be managed and built over time. Find a common bond or thread between you and build on that. It can be something silly, such as both of you love Lucy Ricardo and can sing the theme song to *Grease*. Even this small fact can start your relationship building.

Personal relationships are the fertile soil from which all advancement, all success, all achievement in real life grows.
--Ben Stein

For example, you might have a best friend you met at your last job who you haven't seen in two years. You've been building this relationship for years. If this friend were to call you in the middle of the night, say he was stranded at the airport with no way to get home, and ask you to come get him, you would probably go and pick him up. That is how deep you want your relationships to be. Relationships need to be based on quality, feeling, and trust. Once built on a strong foundation, those relationships will help build your chances of getting the job you want.

There is no such thing as a self-made man. You will reach your goals only with the help of others.
--George Shinn

You need to build 100 of these strong relationships. When you take time to build relationships in a strong manner, you will find all the connections you ever need. Maslow's law of building relationships with people states that you need a few basic things: air, water, food, sex, shelter, and significance. Everyone needs to feel significant in their lives. Connecting with people and giving them significance in your life allows you to expand your relationships.

Making Connections Anywhere

I recently gave a keynote speech at a local church. When the event was over, several people approached me to tell me the speech inspired them. They had no idea you could develop a human connection using LinkedIn. One individual made me stop and think. This individual had been in transition for a while and all she said was, "You gave me hope." She gets it. My passion for LinkedIn is based on the connections you make, which might give you the answers you've been searching for, gain you an interview, or give you hope on a day you need it. You never know when the very next connection you make might open the door.

LinkedIn helps you search your email

in   Search for people, jobs, companies, and more...   Q

Home   Profile   Network   Jobs   Interests

Is Your Business Listed Correctly Online? Check Now For

Quickly grow your professional network
Join Robert, Alan H. and 2,370 others who have found people they already know.

debra.faris@gmail.com

Continue   Your email is safe with us!
We will not store your password or
email anyone without your permission.

Who should I invite?

Have you ever heard the term "fishbowl"? And no, I don't mean the bowl that your goldfish swim around in! Everyone has a fishbowl. Your fishbowl is your network of 10 to 100 friends and family members who like you, respect you, and support you.

As you build your LinkedIn connections, make sure you build connections to your fishbowl, your 10 to 100 incredibly awesome people. One of the ways to do this is to find people they need to connect with. When you find such a connection, send it to them. They will open it and say, "Oh thank you!" It takes less than five seconds. It also takes less than five seconds to let your connections know you were thinking about them.

On each of your connections' profiles, next to the "Send a Message" button, you will find a bucket filled with actions you can take. One of them is "Share your Profile." If you find information on someone's profile that's beneficial to one of your connections, click the share button to send the profile to them. You can also use the button to follow up on someone you are not connected with yet but who you might want to connect with. These little bookmarks can make quite a difference for you.

You never get a second chance to make a first impression.
--Will Rogers

Pieces to the Puzzle: Memory Jogger

For me a memory jogger is like pieces to a puzzle. We all have different ways to put a puzzle together. Most people turn all the pieces over and sometimes section them by color. Other people like to use the box as a guide and work from the outside in. When putting your list together, the memory jogger can help you find people that you know but that you wouldn't immediately consider for inclusion.

The Memory Jogger		
People in your Community		
Tax Person	Fireman	Church
Policeman	Insurance Agent	Dentist

Car Dealer	School Teacher	Dry Cleaner
Hair Dresser	Mechanic	Plumber
Babysitter/Daycare	Chiropractor	Gardener
Pediatrician/Doctor		
Sports		
Golf	Bowling	Water Sports
Hunting	Football	Tennis
Baseball/Softball	Basketball	
Hobbies		
Cooking	Book Club	Music
Hiking	Traveling	
Life Events		
Weddings	Birthdays	
Employment		
Summer Jobs	Internships	
Clubs and Groups		
Corporate Alliances	Tennis club	Fraternity
Academic Decathlon	Sorority	
Multi-Cultural Student Leaders	Honors Programs	Leadership
Best Buddies		
School Acquaintances		
Elementary	Junior High	High School
College	Yearbook	

Should I accept anyone?

How many connections do I need? In a way, yes, there is a magic number. And the magic number is 500. It's like a bad haircut. You don't want people to think you don't have enough. Your results on LinkedIn will only be as good as the quality and variety of the connections you develop. You might get more results with 200 very close connections that resonate with you than with 2,000 connections that are just names.

You can have anything you want – if you want it badly enough. You can be anything you want to be, have anything you desire, accomplish anything you set out to accomplish – if you will hold to that desire with singleness of purpose.
--Robert Collier

"Should I accept anyone who wants to connect?" The answer is simple. Think of accepting connections as like going to a party. You will find people you already know and are connected to. Then you'll meet people who form an instant connection with you. These are the people you know you like from the moment you start talking to them. Then you have the people that you don't connect with, don't like, and don't want to continue talking to. Your LinkedIn connections work the same way. Use your intuition to know if this is someone that you want to have in your circle. If someone doesn't seem right for you and your career path, don't accept the invitation. If you like the person and want to get to know more about them and what they do, connect with them and begin the conversation.

For some of you, accepting everyone will be fun and exciting as you build a huge network to draw on when the time comes. For others, your network may be more limited but more intimate, allowing in only those you're comfortable with and have built great relationships with. Both scenarios are effective. They work in different ways for different people.

Everyone has a purpose in life ... a unique gift of special talent to give others. And when we blend this unique talent with service to others, we experience the ecstasy and exultation of our own spirit, which is the ultimate goal of all goals.
--Deepak Chopra

One key question to ask is, "How much variety is there in my connections?" If you are self-employed, you might look for self-employed connections and pay attention to only the similarities between you and them. The smart person says, "I don't see the similarities between us, I see the differences." This is important because those differences mean that they have many connections you don't have. One of their connections might be a former CEO who could help with your job search.

It is in your moments of decision that your destiny is shaped.
--Tony Robbins

Our first inclination is to look for those like us. Often as human beings, we stay inside our own circles and gravitate towards people who are similar to us. However, a richer and more satisfying experience is possible if we include our opposites in our circle. Think outside the box and connect with people whom you can help or can help you. If you want to show off your musical talents, connect with bands, orchestras, the entertainment industry, schools, anything you can think of where music is important. Think outside the box and your possibilities will be endless.

When you connect with a person, always allow them to see all your contacts, because that creates a measure of trust with the people you connect with. It's silly to hide your contacts, because that means you don't want to play the game. If you share your contacts and they're already in your fishbowl, your new connection may reciprocate, and you may find people that will fit into your fishbowl among their contacts.

Here are This Chapter's Business Consultant Influencers

As you read these profiles, look for possible referrals for your needs.

Is there something in their story you connect with?
Could you gain a new idea or insight for your business or career?
Who do you know or who do they know that can help both of you?
If you needed help or wanted to buy a product, what would it be?
How do you follow up when you meet someone?
When people view your profile, how do you want them to feel?
Do your tribes line up so you could be Power Partners?
What are your favorite questions to ask in an introductory call?

Kurt Glasgow

CEO Glasgow and Associates

"No guts, no glory." ~ *Major General Frederick C. Blesse*

I was born to an Air Force Veteran, and my mother passed away from cancer when I was 2 years old. My Father sent me to live with my grandmother until I was 11. When I moved back to NY I discovered that my dad was getting remarried to a woman with 2 children. At 16 my stepmother gave my Dad an ultimatum that either I needed leave, or she would. My dad chose to send me to a shelter, and I spent the next 2 years taking care of myself & going back & forth from the shelter to the streets.

By 18 years old I was tired of living on the NY streets & decided to follow in my father's footsteps & join the Military where I became a Navy Parachute Rigger. I was deployed on the USS Enterprise to England, Spain, France, Portugal, Greece, Italy & to the coast of Africa. Then came 9-11 causing our 6 month-deployment to increase to 9 months rerouting us from Africa to Afghanistan. These experiences helped me to become the man I am.

Today, I'm a branding & marketing expert who helps clients take their brand to the next level. I'm loved & connected to many influential professionals in the vast network I built. I produce events including Tboz Unplugged, the City Gala & Summit, Higher Xperience, the Arts 4 Peace Awards & concerts for legends like Snoop Dogg & more.

SPECIALTIES: Marketing Expert, Branding Expert, Builder of Long-Term Positive Relationships, Event Production, Billboard Marketing, Commercials, Funding, Concert Production, Award Production

1. **What three books do you feel are a must that you highly recommend others to read?**

Outwitting the Devil, Rich Dad Poor Dad, Think and Grow Rich

2. **What discipline could someone learn from you?**

LOVE, how to naturally connect with someone in the moment.

3. If you could have any superpower (or be any superhero), what/who would it be and why?

I would like to have the ability to time travel & relive amazing moments anytime I want.

4. What subject or argument most stirs your emotions, why?

War, Taxes and Marriage. I believe in Oneness which means no Taxes, Borders, or Governing Institutions tracking people thru the Census. I believe that everyone should work & live as one.

5. When "winning someone over" do you think facts or emotions carry the day?

Facts & honesty are always the best versus telling someone what they want to hear.

6a. What do you wish you spent more time doing?

I'd like to spend more time with my children to create amazing moments & memories for them.

6b. What prevents you from doing that now?

In order to build them a secure future, I need to continually make new connections by going to events.

7. If there were one problem in the world you could solve, what would it be?

I believe that war is the world's biggest problem, and it's mainly caused by people identifying themselves by a label or nationality. I would create a TRUE ONE WORLD GOVERNMENT, destroy all weapons & let people police themselves.

Kurt's Favorite Characteristics

Charisma, Passion, Team Player, Investor
Business Minded, Influencer, Creative, Relationship Builder
Kurt Glasgow aka "Next Level Marketing & Branding Coach"
"Go from Local to Global Overnight,
It just takes One Connection"

♛ Premier Producer, Marketer & Branding Professional ♛ Proven Marketing & Branding Expert ♛ Experienced People Connector to Fund Projects ☎ 424-646-0195 ♟ kurt@TruPassions.com ♛

Learning 2.0

The more I search, the more I find,

The more I find, the more I read,

The more I read, the more I think,

The more I think, the more I learn,

The more I learn, the more I do,

The more I do, the more I create,

The more I create, the more I share,

The more I share, the more I collaborate,

The more I collaborate, the more I connect,

The more I connect, the more I learn,
the more I KNOW

And the more Intelligent

I GROW!

Cheryl Capozzoli

Chapter 4
To Engage or Not to Engage

Your smile will give you a positive countenance that will make people feel comfortable around you.
--Les Brown

Albenago Arseo Jr.

President
A2M Consulting, LLC

My Influencers: Albenago "Al" Arseo

As the networker that I am, I find that people I meet at charities and galas are great ways to build nice relationships. I was at Kiss the Monkeys, which is put on by my friends Al Harris & Raquel Sanchez, who create very high-end galas in Beverly Hills. I met this vivacious beautiful redhead who said she loves volunteering. As we got to talking, I discovered she was in the Air Force. Later while I was working the event, I asked if she knew anyone who hired Veterans and that is how I met Al Arseo

Al is the President/CEO of A2M Consulting, LLC. He told me, "My job is to bring business opportunities to the company and build business relationships with other DoD companies large and small. Our four-revenue streams concentrate in the areas of Administration,

Aircrew training, Information technology and Aircraft Maintenance."

"I heard you were in the Air Force," I said.

"I joined the Air Force in January 1981 so I could provide better health care, housing and food for my small family. At the time I was working as a machinist apprentice in Riverside, CA. I had married my high school sweetheart in 1980 and she was pregnant with our first child"

"How did the Air Force help you build your career?"

"I started as Crew Chief on the largest aircraft in the Air Force inventory. As my career progressed, I continued to work in the aircraft maintenance field."

"That's quite a start," I said.

"It was amazing," he said. "As the years went by, I progressed through the ranks, received my Associates degree, bachelor's degree and Airframe Power plant License. Later, after 23 years I became a Chief Master Sergeant, the highest enlisted rank attainable. After 28 years serving in the Air Force, I retired. I then transitioned to the Defense Contracting sector and worked for a fortune 500 company, SAIC. After a year and a half, I opened my own Small Business company and 10 years later we are still in business."

Who Viewed You?

Do you remember the story of *The Tortoise and the Hare*? What about the phrase, "Slow and steady wins the race?" In this fable from childhood, the moral is that being persistent and taking things one step at a time will get you the results you desire. One of the 12 traits of over-achievers outlined in one of the most famous books in personal development history, *Think & Grow Rich* by Napoleon Hill, is to take small steps every day to accomplish your goals. The Tortoise who schedules five minutes every day will progress farther than the Hare who creates a burst of energy every few weeks. If you spend five minutes a day on LinkedIn, you will be like the early bird that gets the worm.

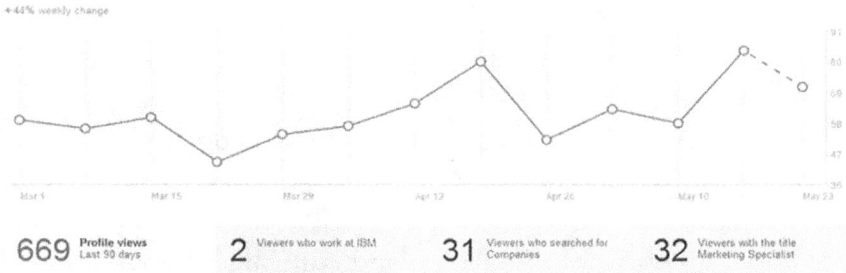

One of the most important tasks you can do in your five minutes a day is look at the five most recent persons to view your LinkedIn profile. This is a great advantage LinkedIn provides since no other websites give you that information. With this information, you can now view that person's profile and learn more about them.

First, look at how you are connected to them (if at all). Note the common traits, desires, and goals you share. Then look at what you do not share with this person. If you share nothing, there is always potential for you to be their opposite.

Shoot for the moon and if you miss you will still be among the stars.
--Les Brown

This person viewed you for a reason and that starts to forge a connection between the two of you, again for a reason. Even if you have nothing in common with this person, you should either send them an invite to connect or share their profile with someone you think would connect well with them. Helping other people today will make their tomorrow better and they will remember you in your future.

Shared Connections Are Gold

Earlier, I showed you how to identify the 10 to 100 most important people in your life. These are the people you invite to your wedding or who will attend your funeral, the people who are most visible in your life and in many cases the most likely to help you in time of need.

Although you want to develop and cultivate all your LinkedIn connections, these 100 people may hold the key to your future. You need to build a connection with them at an emotional level, both one-on-one and in a group. People don't care about how much you know until they know how much you care. Spend time and energy fostering a strong relationship with these individuals. From there, you can build more distant connections and share your most important connections with people who would appreciate knowing them. It's important to share your connections with others and continue to foster strong relationships.

Lee Shares 164

in

Search for people, jobs, companies, and more...

Connections

Shared (164)

Bob Burg 1st
Bestselling Author & Convention Speaker...

Mari Smith 1st
Facebook Marketing Expert Author & Trai...

Nathan Kievman 1st
CEO Linked Strategies | World Renowne...

Mark Williams 1st
Mark Williams ▶ Independent LinkedIn Tr...

Melissa Giovagnoli (G)Wilson 1st
Social Media & Publishing Expert, Speak...

Paula Constantino 1st
CEO & Coach @ Find A Coach Online ~ ...

Warren Paulins 1st
3775+, Executive Management Professio...

Dave Jauné 1st
Recruiter at KellyOCG

William Giba ITSM 1st
Fortune 500 Consultant at Self-Employed...

Susan Karr 1st
Executive Recruiter at CyberCoders| Sub...

Sharing your connections is simple. When you find a connection that you know someone else can use, move your cursor to the right of the "Send InMail" button and right click; a drop-down menu will appear, select "Share" and follow the steps. The person you are sending the connection to will get a LinkedIn "In Mail" with their profile attached. This is your opportunity to help those that are helping you.

To Endorse or Not to Endorse

In the beginning, when LinkedIn brought endorsements to their platform, I had numerous calls from people confused as to what it was and why someone they didn't know was endorsing them. Some people find change difficult because they don't understand it.

Engage By Endorsements

However, people who were used to Facebook were comfortable with the new addition to LinkedIn since it gave them an opportunity to have an online conversation by acknowledging something they liked about another profile, which they couldn't do anywhere else. I took a deep breath and realized that people's frustration came from a lack of understanding about the value of this new feature. One client I was working with was very confused. I explained to him that it was a compliment. The first question I asked was, "Did you look at your profile and search for the person's name and are they a first level connection?" Out of embarrassment but honesty, he acknowledged they were first connections.

I said, "Do you remember this person?"

After a moment's pause, he scanned the profile and said, "Oh, I remember him."

I asked, "Is there something in his profile that you like that could get the conversation rolling?"

After looking at the profile, he found three things he liked and found a way to do business with the other party. When the ball bounces to your side of the court, it's your turn to give back. You can endorse a skill on his profile or take it one step deeper and send him a LinkedIn message. Within the week, he sent me a thank you back and said he was meeting his new LinkedIn friend in person.

Social media is changing the way we communicate and the way we are perceived, both positively and negatively. Every time you post a photo, or update your status, you are contributing to your own digital footprint and personal brand.
--Amy Jo Martin

When you notice a person with over 99 endorsements, find the skill that's most endorsed on that profile that most resonates with you. Let's say its creativity. When you move your cursor to the right on the line where the photos are, it will show you everyone who has endorsed that person. It's fun to see who your first connections are but another opportunity to grow your LinkedIn connections is to look at level people who you can network with or who can help you build you path to an exciting job.

Positioning and Aligning

When you build your LinkedIn profile, it's important to use your character words with your skills in an alignment that is in harmony with your purpose and intentions. If you want to be promoted to CFO and your profile shows that in previous positions you worked in the sales department but not in accounting, you will confuse those looking at your profile. However, if you worked for the accounting department, even in a support position, you need to make that experience clear.

You position yourself when you find other LinkedIn members who do what you do or what you want to do and connect with them. This begins to build your well. When you're connected to someone who does what you want, other people will see you and you can move into their circles and connect with them.

Here are This Chapter's Business Consultant Influencers

As you read these profiles, look for possible referrals for your needs.

Is there something in their story you connect with?

Could you gain a new idea or insight for your business or career?

Who do you know or who do they know that can help both of you?

If you needed help or wanted to buy a product, what would it be?

How do you follow up when you meet someone?

When people view your profile, how do you want them to feel?

Do your tribes line up so you could be Power Partners?

What are your favorite questions to ask in an introductory call?

Steven Spriggs

The Veterans Loan Officer

"Leadership is a potent combination of strategy and character." Gen. Schwarzkopf

I grew up in a small farm town in Ohio and entered the Army at the age of 20. After serving with the historic Army unit called the "Blackhorse Troopers" in Vietnam, I returned home and resumed my career in harness racing where many of the leading trainers were military veterans and who served as my mentors.

Today, I have worked for 30 years in the mortgage loan industry where I have funded over 7,000 loans in all 50 states!! Beginning with my employment at Ditech/GMAC Mortgage, I felt compelled to mentor my fellow Veterans as I was mentored in harness racing.

► Created a VA platform at Ditech.com, Greenlight Loans and CashCall Mortgage to convert VA loan leads that were being abandoned into profitable, funded loans.

► Trained 90+ Loan Officers to originate VA loans at three mortgage companies.

► While other loan officers blew out deals because they thought the Veteran VA loans were too tough to deal with, I knew the guidelines so I found a way to close loans and not just to create another dead deal. Happy to help fellow veterans get into their home.

SPECIALTIES: Mortgage Lending / Relationship Management / Negotiation / Strategy/ Training / Mentoring Teams for VA Loans / Team Building / Speaking / Community Outreach /Charity / Fundraising /

Military Foundations and Organizations that Support Military Veterans and Families

- Veterans of Foreign Wars, Life Member
- Orange County, CA American Legion Post & County Commander
- Assoc. US Army Greater Los Angeles Chapter, Member
- Heroes Hall Veterans Foundation, Board Member
- Fisher House SoCal Foundation, Board Member
- Veterans Alliance of Orange County (VALOR), Board Member
- Orange County Veterans & Military Families Collaborative, Board Member
- City of Newport Beach 1/1 Marines Foundation, Board Member 2005-2015-
- 11th Armored Cavalry Veterans of Vietnam and Cambodia, Life Member
- Blackhorse Assn. (11th ACR), Life Member

Steve Spriggs aka "The Veteran Loan Officer"

"I Help Veterans Purchase Homes for Their Families"

▶ 949-355-3051 ▶ stevenbspriggs@gmail.com

One of the most powerful

networking practices

is to provide

immediate value

to a new connection.

This means the moment

you identify

a way to help someone,

take action.

Lewis Howes

Chapter 5
Networking to the Next Level

First, you have to be visible in the community. You have to get out there and connect with people. It's not called net-sitting or net-eating. It's called networking. You have to work at it.
-- Ivan Misner

My Influencers: Joe Molina

Joe Molina served in the Army. Recently he said to me, "It was one of the most rewarding times in my life. It was a privileged and a great honor to serve my country and to have the opportunity to protect our freedom. During my time in the Army and while stationed in Alaska, I managed cold weather training programs, my job was to qualify personnel to meet readiness specially under difficult weather. It was a fun job and I guess training and teaching are a part of who I am. I enjoy teaching, whether it is business courses or Leadership Skills for new supervisors. I enjoy sharing knowledge and experience first-hand as students get to the moment when information knowledge turns into learned knowledge."

He emphasized that the Veterans Chamber of Commerce was created out of the desire to empower Veterans and organizations that serve veterans through programs and projects that will support veterans. Its key support areas are entrepreneurship - employment – education, family and wellness. He currently serves as the CEO.

"We also want it to provide a no cost membership for all veterans and organizations, create a mission that will be supported by people with passion for helping veterans. Today, in less than two years we have grown from a single program to 16 different programs that support veterans, all coordinated by people who love what they do and have a strong passion for helping veterans and their families. The years of military experience along with teaching experience at the University, gave me the tools necessary to create the platform that will later become the Veterans Chamber of Commerce."

The mission of the Veterans Chamber of Commerce is to empower organizations and individuals with programs and projects that will positively impact the veteran's community.

"The philosophy of the Chamber is that we seek to work with positive people & with organizations who have a forward vision. We believe in creating strong bonds of collaboration and partnerships with individuals and organizations who share the desire and passion for supporting and empowering the veteran community nation-wide," Molina said.

The website is www.vccsd.org

Your Million Dollar Message

I never thought I needed a pitch when I met people. Then I attended an executive networking group that held a training class once a week. Part of the curriculum to train people who had lost their jobs (in transition) was how to create a pitch. Since I had been in the banking industry for 15 years and the banks were disintegrating, I figured I needed to check this class out. The curriculum taught students how to write a resume, have a mock interview, learn how to network, and to create a 30-second elevator Pitch. They taught that you need to know how to tell people in an instant in a clear and concise manner who you are and what you're looking for. It was a great way for me to sharpen my skills and acquire new ones.

When I stepped into the class, it all seemed so natural for me that they were surprised with my natural unconventional networking manner. They were so impressed that they asked me to be one of the trainers. Two weeks later I stepped into the trainer position and two weeks after that they made me a lead trainer. It was cool being a trainer because I was helping people and at the same time honing my own skills.

One day I worked with a man in his 50s who had been a CFO (Chief Financial Officer) for over 25 years. He had only two jobs in his entire career, was making over a quarter million a year, and had been with the same company for over a dozen years. At the end of one day, I told the class that the next day we would give our 30-second pitch. As I handed him the assignment so he could prepare for the next day, he looked at me with a puzzled expression.

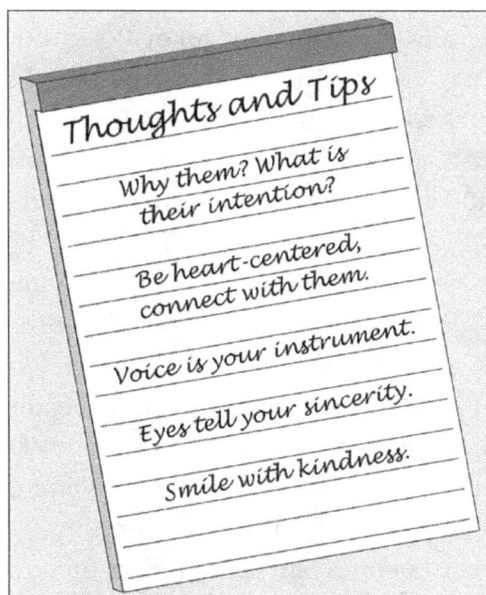

Thoughts and Tips

Why them? What is their intention?

Be heart-centered, connect with them.

Voice is your instrument.

Eyes tell your sincerity.

Smile with kindness.

He showed up the next day and took his seat among the 14 people in the class. I put an example of a 120-word pitch up on the screen. "You need to present this pitch in 30 seconds or less," I said. His face reflected the look of an individual clearly apprehensive about taking on this task, but also determination to give it all he had. He had been a leader all his life, and this C-level executive wanted people to see him as a prospect for any job his new-found peers might know about. I saw hesitation. When his turn came, he stood and started to introduce himself but got so caught up in trying to remember the words that he stuttered and turned 50 shades of red. Did I say that this man was about 6'4" and weighed at least 220 pounds? I'm 5'3" and a little thing next to this big guy.

When the rubber meets the road you just jump in with both feet. I wanted him to know I would be his wingman and together we could do this. I stood next to him. His eyes were filled with tears. It broke my heart to see such a prideful man feel like he was a failure.

I remembered a Tony Robbins seminar I had attended where I learned about pattern interruptions. This would be the perfect time for me to share this technique with the class and make it fun at the same time. I told them, "Let's do the Hokey Pokey and turn ourselves around." They humored me and did the exercise as I instructed them. I could see the confusion on my CFO's face.

When we finished, I said, "Now, tell everyone what industry you are most interested in and tell everyone one thing that you could do to help them."

The man, now much more at ease, told everyone that he would be happy to help any of the class members by introducing them to any of his LinkedIn contacts. He then added that it would be an honor to do so and that his name was John Smith. He ended his 30-second pitch with, "Thank you very much. It's nice to meet all of you." The class jumped to their feet and gave him a standing ovation. It made me feel like I had made a huge difference for him.

In this situation, the man had shifted from thinking with his head to feeling with his heart. He functioned from a place of laughter and compassion.

When teaching you to create your own pitch, trainers will tell you, "Stand in front of the mirror and go blah, blah, blah." An even better option is to talk to a doll or teddy bear or the cutest thing you ever saw. When we talk to ourselves in the mirror we were talking from our heads. When we talk to another object, we are talking from our hearts. You shift into your being, your conversations, your body, and your caring. You come from laughter and compassion. You shift and your pitch shifts with you.

That's what needs to happen on your LinkedIn. When you shift from being all about me to being all about what they need, everything shifts for you.

You also need to shift your conversations from your body to being and caring. On your LinkedIn profile, shift from thinking about yourself and what you can get out of a connection to thinking about what you can do for the other person. You will forge real connections where you will find true benefits. If you aren't thinking about whom your audience is, they may be repelled by what you have to say. If you pay attention to them, you will tailor the conversation that honors who they are. That will get you connections that matter.

F.O.R.M.

A lot of people ask me, "How do I network? How do I know who, when, where and how?" It is easy to figure this out, because people are attracted to like-minded people who share a common taste in things such as clothing, hobbies and careers.

When you understand this, you can learn to network any time anywhere. I learned this process in a network marketing company and it is still used all over the world in many companies. You can use it every day whether you are sitting in a dentist's office or you are networking at a social event.

The "Who am I" who shows up is your integrity, your loyalty, your dependability, your creativity, all the human character traits that you bring to your networking.

The acronym for this process is F.O.R.M.

F is for where they are From. I also like to ask where they were born. I have found that many people have known their friends for many years but never knew whether these friends came from a place they had in common or had a place they always wanted to explore.

O is for your Occupation. Asking a new connection what industry they work in is important both for someone who is in transition or someone who already works for a company.

R is your Recreation. A lot of people like to talk about their hobbies and what they do on weekends.

M is your Message. Your message is how you can help potential employers when you are looking for a job.

From: You ask your new connection two questions, "Where are you from?" and "Where were you born?" You wait for the answers, take two seconds to pause. After you give your connection the opportunity to share where they are from, reflect back to them where you were born and where you live. You may discover you have something in common.

Occupation: What do you do or what industry are you in? Remember, if your connection is in transition and the networking event is about job-hunting, stick to mentioning your industry and don't add who you work for. Reflect back to them the parts of your career that complement their past or present career.

Recreation: You may meet someone at a social gathering or fun event. It is easy to start a conversation about the hobbies, sports, or other fun things. Reflect commonalities between you, which will build a bond as each of you discovers more about the other.

Message: Now that you have established rapport, you can share that you are on LinkedIn and would be happy to help them with some of your connections. Ask yourself, "What is the one key thing that I could ask if they need help with."

Qualify like a CEO

Let's say you have become a CFO who works in Los Angeles, but you commute 50 miles from Orange County and you would like to find a job closer to home in Orange County.

> *If you're not making mistakes, then you're not doing anything. I'm positive that a doer makes mistakes.*
> **--John Wooden**

One ideal way to make that happen is find a referring partner. First you go to LinkedIn and find a CFO that's in transition and ask him to visit you in Orange County. You sit down for breakfast or lunch with this partner and say, "You're a CFO and I'm a CFO and my wife would be very unhappy if we moved out of Orange County because our kids and our church are here. I know that you want to work in Los Angeles and I want to work in Orange County. How about sharing leads? I can give you leads I hear about in Los Angeles and you can share Orange County leads with me."

> *I have a dream that my four little children will one day live in a nation where they will not be judged by the color of their skin, but by the content of their character.*
> **--Martin Luther King, Jr.**

Remember that people are people and have needs to take care of. If you eliminate the fear that you might take away another person's position, you now have as a partner a 100% invested person that has the same goal as you. Working together and networking in your respective areas, you can help each other be successful.

Networking Tips

1. Keep your body language open if you want to get to know someone. Hold your shoulders a little bit back. When you shake their hand, look them in the eye.

2. When you are at a networking event where you want to meet people, everybody has a comfort zone. If you sense you are too close based on the other person's reaction, step back. They are telling you that you are in their space. It's nothing to be offended over, just give them more space.

3. Networking is about getting out of your head and into your heart.

4. People need to feel comfortable with who you are and how you show up.

5. When you network, you change hats depending on your audience. You wouldn't talk in a business office like you would talk at a baseball game. You think from your audience's perspective.

6. When you smile, you show another of your human sides and people will feel comfortable with you.

7. Remember to keep your questions light. People don't like to feel that they are being interrogated.

8. Keep your conversations and your body in a caring posture. Come from laughter and compassion.

9. Sometimes we can give too much information about ourselves and then people make judgments.

10. When all else fails and you don't know who to talk to, look for the guy or gal who is standing alone and seems to be thinking, "Why am I here?" He knows why he's there. He just doesn't know how to approach other people. So be the hero and start conversations with F.O.R.M.

What is Left-Brain Right-Brain connecting?

I'm sure you've heard the terms "Left-Brained" and "Right-Brained" before, but have you ever considered the depth of the terms' meaning? A Left-Brained individual is a person who utilizes mostly the left side of their brain, making that individual more analytical, logical, and objective. A Right-Brained individual uses mostly the right side of their brain, which leads to a more subjective, thoughtful, and intuitive approach.

Left-Brain dominant individuals typically fill roles such as CFO (Chief Financial Officer) and COO (Chief Operating Officer) due to their analytical capabilities. Right-Brain dominant individuals typically fill roles such as CMO (Chief Marketing Officer), CNO (Chief Networking Officer) and CEO (Chief Executive Officer), although these people can fall into either category depending on whether they were appointed or founded the company.

When I work with C-level Left-Brained dominant individuals who love equations and analytics, I find that trying to get them to do anything creative or unorthodox makes them uncomfortable. When I work with the Right-Brained dominant individuals, who love creativity, they get lost in the massive amount of information analytics provides. It dawned on me that the perfect pairing was to match Left-Brained and Right-Brained persons, who will then complement each other perfectly and produce both the analysis and the creativity that successful companies and people require.

This concept also works when two opposite individuals work together on LinkedIn. The "Right-Brain" dominant person can create a more attractive profile while the "Left-Brained" dominant individual can create more detailed content and catch errors that are not obvious. When two people from opposite sides of the coin get together, they will produce a more balanced and robust LinkedIn profile. This pertains to writing a profile and also works amazingly well in person when connecting with another human being.

Character isn't something you were born with and can't change, like your fingerprints. It's something you weren't born with and must take responsibility for forming.
--Jim Rohn

A Left-Brained individual may stand in a corner and analyze the room. They might come from a place of judgment versus the place of observation the Right-Brained individual prefers. Each will communicate in different styles and operate in different styles. Yet when they work together, they complement each other and help each other by introducing new contacts they could not have discovered alone. This is a great way to network since the Left-Brained individual is good with detail and can be a great accountability partner for the Right-Brained individual. Each will open doors for the other, creating a perfectly balanced networking team.

Try this out by meeting at least three people who are your opposites the next time you go to a networking event. If you are an extrovert, look for someone who is more introverted. If you are creative, look for a good organizer. If you think you are introverted and not a networker, look for the friendliest person in the room and start a conversation. You will meet your exact opposite, the very person you need to meet, because when the two of you come together you never know what might happen.

The Deeper You Go, the Closer You Get to Gold

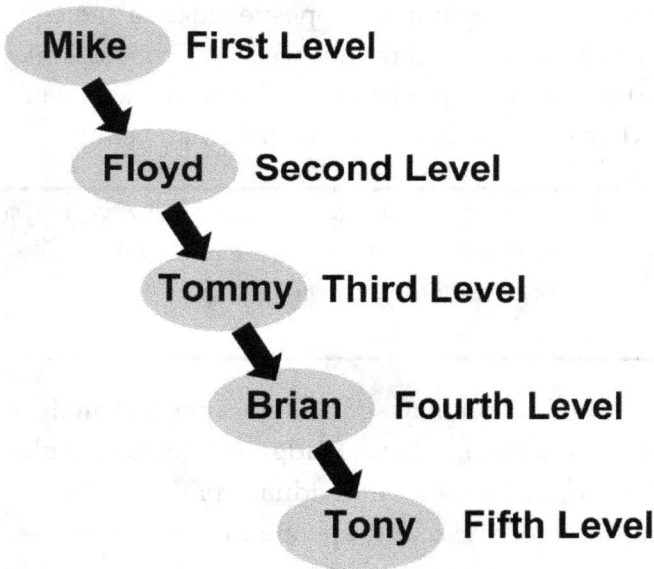

Mike **First Level**

Floyd **Second Level**

Tommy **Third Level**

Brian **Fourth Level**

Tony **Fifth Level**

Go Deep in Your Connections

In the book *Think and Grow Rich*, Napoleon Hill tells the story of R. U. Darby, a Maryland businessman who discovered a rich vein of gold in the Colorado Mountains. They followed the vein until it gave out. Certain that no more gold existed, they quit and sold out to a junk dealer, who found a new vein of gold just three feet away from where Darby had stopped. The junk man made millions. I want to share with you, many people give up when they are only three feet away!

In social media it is a common to hear people say, "Six Degrees to Kevin Bacon" phrase, because people realized that through this person they could ask someone do you know someone who knows Kevin Bacon and then they would continue to ask so on and so forth. In theory, this means everyone in the world is connected to everyone else in the world by a chain of no more than six people. This was shown in the movie, *Six Degrees of Separation* with Kevin Bacon. With LinkedIn I have found people with three or four searches. The closer the alignment the closer you are to finding them.

With a few searches on LinkedIn, you can find almost anyone you want to connect with because LinkedIn can link you to 300 million of the billions of people on our planet.

Network Like Your Life Depends on It

When a recruiter or an influential individual meets they will mentally place you in one of four buckets: Yes. No. Maybe.!

The key to coming across as a potential partner, he says, is to use confidence and communication skills (both are skills that can be learned!) to stand out from the crowd and building *personal relationships* with influential individuals. The key includes having a range of diversity within your network.

For example, if you are Salesperson, it's important to develop relationships with individuals who are in other disciplines who have different values and perspectives, such as Accounting or

Engineering. This diversity in networks is beneficial for a variety of reasons:

1. It enables you to be a connector who can bring two usually separate groups of people together.

2. It allows you to be more self-aware and open-minded by understanding a diversity of viewpoints

3. It exposes you to opportunities that you may not be aware of

"It's not always easy to build a relationship with a person who is different from you," Jaymin Patel says. "However, it's easier than you might think. Use my Three Word Intro, which goes like this: 'Hi, I'm Jaymin.'"

This approach works 99% of the time, he says. "When the other person does not respond it's ok. Just use the Three Word Intro on the next person! For best results, use it in an environment common to the individual you are speaking with."

Once Jaymin used the Three Word Intro on a plane. That stranger became one of the most impactful individuals in his career. "He connected me with an opportunity I wasn't aware of," he said. "I left my full-time job and became an author, speaker, and coach reaching thousands around the world."

He added, "When you know how to start a conversation with anyone, you can build diversity into your network by networking like a ROCKSTAR!"

Who are the top 10 most powerful connections you have? The people who can make things happen for you! Then ask yourself, what have I done for these people lately? Or, maybe a better question is, are these people you just call every once in a while to suck their blood.
--Jeffrey Gitomer

Relationship Currency

Relationship Currency is such an interesting topic. When he speaks about relationship bank accounts Steven Covey says, "First seek to understand then to be understood." If you had an account that had $1,000 and all you did was take money out and never to make any deposits, it wouldn't be too long before it was empty. There used to be a saying save your pennies for a rainy day (now it would be dollars). However, there are some people who will ask again and again for things and we may feel like they never give anything in return. The same goes on in networking and on LinkedIn. People will ask for a recommendation and they have never even made another point of communication after the initial invite, not alone a phone call but they want you to recommend them? It's kind of confusing especially when you are new, and you want to build someone relationships. So how do you build your own LinkedIn currency? Here are a few tips:

1. Looking through your new updates and when you see one of your new connections got a job, send them congratulations.

2. Someone has a new photo, tell them you noticed.

3. You see a new member in a group, go look at their profile and then send them a welcome to the group with a nice comment about their profile and send them a welcome with a nice comment

4. When you see a job that is in the industry of one of your top 20 send them the Link of forward them the job posting.

5. When you see a charity on one of your friend's profiles, ask them more about it.

Go confidently in the direction of your dreams. Live the life you have imagined.
--Henry David Thoreau

How to Win Friends and Influence People

Sometimes life comes full circle. One of the very first leadership training courses I took was Dale Carnegie. At the time I didn't know Mr. Carnegie had passed before I was born. The core values and principles he taught are timeless. Many years later in Vegas, I attended Author 101 heard Jill Lublin, author of the best seller *Networking Magic* speak.

Later that afternoon I bumped into her in the hall, had a nice chat, and exchanged cards, just enjoying our moment together and connecting. I thanked her for her words of wisdom.

Later I looked her up on LinkedIn and discovered she was a modern-day Dale Carnegie on how to be influential. She's been featured in the New York Times, Women's Day, Fortune, Small Business, Inc., and Entrepreneur Magazine, and on ABC, CBS, NBC TV and radio. When your values align with other great peoples values it creates a strong foundation for new relationships.

Here's one of Jill's tried and true philosophies:

---

*Without introductions, matches can't be made.

*Without matches, connections cannot be created.

*Without connections, bonds cannot form

*Without bonding, relationships cannot be built and

*Without reciprocal relationships, networks cannot last

*Continue to grow your friendships to the next level.

Here are This Chapter's Business Consultant Influencers

As you read these profiles, look for possible referrals for your needs.

Is there something in their story you connect with?

Could you gain a new idea or insight for your business or career?

Who do you know or who do they know that can help both of you?

If you needed help or wanted to buy a product, what would it be?

How do you follow up when you meet someone?

When people view your profile, how do you want them to feel?

Do your tribes line up so you could be Power Partners?

What are your favorite questions to ask in an introductory call?

Thomas Evans

**Founder & President at
The Home Owner Alliance**

I am an ambitious Search Engine Marketing professional in the Internet Marketing industry. I specialize in organic Search Engine Optimization, new business sales, business development, and, client SEM education to maximize productivity and ROI. My professional experience in SEO includes site analysis, on-page and off-page optimization, SEM strategy development and targeted content development for client websites. I improve online visibility with every client I work with. My experience includes multiple clients from various industries throughout the United States and Canada.

Networking360 was created to bring the true Professionals around The Phoenix-Metro area together to create new relationships, partnerships and help EVERYONE grow their business.

Headquartered in Scottsdale, AZ, GetFoundAgent.com was established with the intent to provide online marketing solutions to Real Estate Agents.

GetFoundAgent.com offers an affordable Real Estate Website platform that can generate quality Buyer/Seller leads provided with SEO (Search Engine Optimization) services, Social Media Ads, and or PPC (Pay-Per-Click) campaigns.

ThomasEvanbs

linkedin.com/in/thomasevansgetfoundrealtor

Website getfoundagent.com (Company Website)

Phone (602) 571-2999 (Mobile)

Email tevans@networking360az.com

We all construct worldviews
that give us a sense of meaning.

Mostly it is about
belonging to a group
and having a sense
of identity and purpose.

Carmen Lawrence

Chapter 6
Groups, Tribes, and
Communities

There are 7 billion on the planet. There's enough business for everyone.
--Sandra Yancey

Stacy Sanchez

CEO at American Veterans Group

My Influencers: Stacy Sanchez

Most people do not know that there are over 2 million groups on LinkedIn. When I was looking for a group that served Veterans, I found Stacy Sanchez at American Veterans Group in Long Beach that provides in-home care to Veterans. We share over 389 connections.

When we met, he said, "Our corporate focus is Military Veterans who are in need. As a prior Marine, I know how important this is. We spend a lot of energy and resources finding benefits for our Veterans that are entitled to them but have issues getting access to them. We have assisted over 1000 Vets in our time being in business."

"Tell me why you joined the service?" I asked him.

"My father was the biggest influencer in my life. To me he was made of granite and 10 feet tall, was an immigrant from Mexico and loved this country. When allowed to join the military, he jumped at the opportunity. US Army said yes first, so he joined the Army as an infantry man and was shipped to Vietnam. While serving in Vietnam, my father did his country proud and was awarded 3 Purple Hearts, A Silver Star, 2 Bronze stars and the Soldiers Medal."

"What did he do after that?"

"That's the sad part. My father valiantly served our country. When he went to re-enlist, the Medical Doctor informed him he had been exposed to Agent Orange and it manifested itself as Leukemia. The Army gave my father a medical Honorable discharge and 8 years later he died of his Leukemia. I was with my dad every one of those days of those 8 years. We made the best of every day."

"So you have a tradition of service."

"Both my grandfathers served in the military, my father served, uncles served, my brother served and I served. It was our family business. It was only a natural transition for me to join the military after High School. While in US Marine Corps bootcamp, MCRD, I set the US Marine Corps sit up record that had held for the last 40 years and graduated a proud US Marine Corps, Infantryman."

"What was the most valuable thing you got out of the service?"

"Being a US Marine builds character and perseverance, but the Special Forces of the highest trained military, took it to a whole other level. The Marines Corps taught me brotherhood, teamwork, leadership, taught me the ability to improvise and above all else, taught me to never give up and to always accomplish my mission, no matter what that be. I will die a proud US Marine."

"What do you do today?"

"I am honored and privileged to own two in-home Care companies. Each 100% serves our military Veterans. One, **Veterans Wellness Services Inc** is a state non-profit agency that assists Veterans with applying for and receiving military benefits they are entitled to. The 2nd company is **American Veterans Group**, a for profit California licensed In-Home Care company that has had the honor over the last 10 years of providing In-Home Care to over 2000 Veterans for over 1,250,000 hours of care that include bathing, ambulating, cooking for, laundry, housekeeping and transportation to our most needed Veterans. We provide care only to the prior substance addicted, the homeless and the lowest income Veterans in Southern California

"As a military Veterans, we have an insight and view of our Veterans that those that have not served my not quite fully grasp. I am honor bound to provide care to my brothers and sisters that have previously served our country. It is my pleasure."

One of my favorite of her quotes is "NO is an acronym for Next Opportunity!" It's always been a great survival value for people to believe they belong to a superior tribe. That's just in human relationships.
--E. O. Wilson

Seven Ways to Pick a Group

Being part of the right group has always been an important part of our identity and is an important part of LinkedIn as well. Being associated with the right group can help you land the right job!

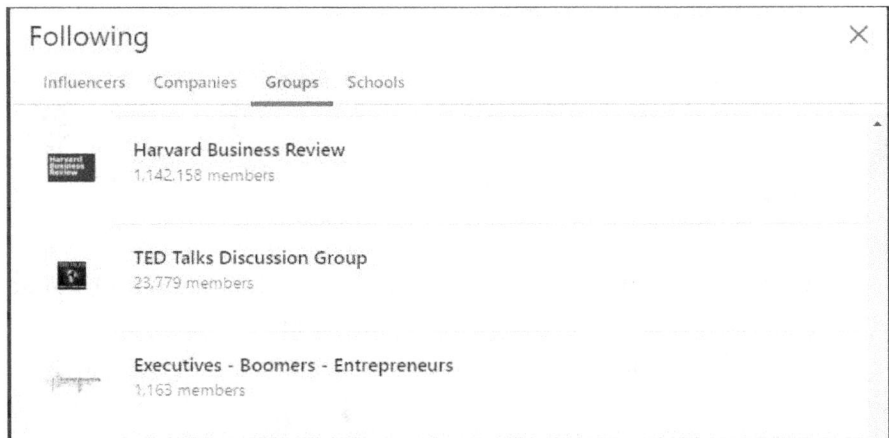

Following   ✕

Influencers   Companies   **Groups**   Schools

Harvard Business Review
1,142,158 members

TED Talks Discussion Group
23,779 members

Executives - Boomers - Entrepreneurs
1,163 members

If you look at Mike Ferry™'s LinkedIn page, you will see that he has joined a lot of groups that include realtors. This makes a lot of sense if, like Mike, you are one of the top real estate professional trainers in the world. However, it makes no sense at all if you are a real estate agent. Many agents make a huge mistake when they create their LinkedIn profiles. They join groups made up of other realtors. They think that by being visible in the realtor community, they will attract customers. What is the mistake? When you do this, other realtors will find you and look at your profile. Nobody else will. The most important question you can ask yourself, the question that means everything for you and your business, is, "Is a realtor going to sell a house to another realtor?" Rephrase this question so it applies to your business.

Showing 2,635 results

US Military Veterans Network
86,908 members

US Veterans
65,397 members

Iraq War Veterans
31,028 members

Army Veterans
58,063 members

Searching for groups is very simple on LinkedIn. The search bar allows you the find People, Updates, Jobs, Companies, your Inbox, or Groups. You want to make Groups your default. Just change your settings.

LinkedIn is home to over 2,000,000 groups. Groups representing every industry, hobby, life interest and passion can be found on LinkedIn. Picking a group is like picking music. With so many genres available, it is critical that you chose the ones that fit your purpose in your profession but also in your personality and gifts. Here are some options:

What tribes are is a very simple concept that goes back 50 million years. It's about leading and connecting people and ideas. And it's something that people have wanted forever.

--Seth Godin

US Military Veterans Network
Standard group

86,908 members   Request to join

About this group

This is an exclusive, all volunteer force of US Military Veterans. If you have served in one of the US Military branches, enlisted or officer, you are welcome to join (please include veteran experience in profile). We are interested in serving the needs of veterans in Life, Politics and Business.

1. **Group Size - Papa Bear, Mama Bear, and Baby Bear:** (this is a fun metaphor that I use to remember group size)

   A. The first thing you want to select when you are picking a group is to pick a huge group, the Papa Bear
   B. Then pick a medium-sized group, the Mama Bear
   C. Then add a small group, the Baby Bear

2. **Fun-Fun-Fun**: Of the 2,000,000 groups on LinkedIn, pick a fun, exciting group that makes you think, "Wow, if I could do this for a living, this would be fun."

3. Recruit Me. I want a job: Find out where all the Human Resources people, recruiters and headhunters play. Seek them out and speak to them.

4. People like Me: Find groups with people like you that you can ask, "What works for you and what doesn't."

5. Who are your Top 25? Look at their groups and join groups that make sense for you.

6. Job Groups, Headhunters, and Recruiters: Joining these groups is the key to successful searches for recruiters who live in your community or are recruiters for your industry or field

← US Veteran - Recruiter - Candidate Connection

6,700 Members   🔍 Search members

Rob Barrett · 1st   **Owner**
Director of Recruiting and all things Social - Chameleon - Bringing People Together   Message

Michael Leitschuh · 2nd   **Manager**
Senior IT Recruiter   Message

Ed Lechner · 2nd   **Manager**
Facility Security Officer / Senior Technical Recruiter at Chameleon Integrated Services - elechner@chameleonis.com   Message

Les Davis, USA(ret) · 1st
Director of Military Admissions at Spartan College of Aeronautics and Technology   Message

7. Top Link: I have saved the Best for Last. This open Networkers Group (TopLink.com) has 138,000 members. If you are not yet a member, you can click the "Join Group" button. This open networker group includes some of the very largest connectors on LinkedIn, many of whom have many thousands of connections. When you first join this group, let the Open Networkers Logo show up on your profile since it might attract more connections interested in what you do. In the future, however, when you reach a higher level on LinkedIn and want to show only high-quality groups in your profile, do not show the TopLink Logo because it means that you're an open connector. If want to keep your connections more private and want them to look at you as a careful connector with special people, you don't want them to know you are an open networker.

Do make it a practice to explore the many groups on LinkedIn. Before you join any group, you can see the members of the group who are in your network and in some groups, you can read discussion threads. At the very least, you can see who the group owner is, how many members the group has, and whether it is open or closed. Once you join, you can see the other people who belong to the group.

When you see the five or six connections of yours that are members of the new group, you might think, "Oh my goodness, all of these people are first connections with me. These individuals have (for instance) painting careers but I'm not in this group with them." If you see that six of your first level connections are in this art group and you are interested in art, you might want to pursue stronger connections with those people."

You do want to join the maximum of 50 groups because when you are in a group, you can send up to 15 emails per month to individual members of a group without being connected to them. This adds a few more people who can send you a message. However, work just the top three of these groups strongly so you do not make extra work for yourself. Work smarter, not harder.

What's a tribe?

If you look up the word "tribe" in the dictionary you will get this definition: a social division in a traditional society consisting of families or communities linked by social, economic, religious, or blood ties, with a common culture and dialect, typically having a recognized leader.

Your most important job on LinkedIn is to find others in your field. Begin by looking at 100 people who do what you do on LinkedIn. You will see how they target their tribe and you will find good connections who could refer business to you. I've looked at thousands of profiles, so I have a good idea what a successful profile contains. If you haven't looked at your first 100 people, then you have no idea who is out there and who can help you.

In order to effect great change, we need to look at how we can help those in our own communities as well as globally.
--Christina Aguilera

Keep a notebook labeled *Tips and Ideas for LinkedIn*. When you find people who might be good connections, make a note of them. Write down how that person resonates with you and what that person might mean to you. Then connect with them.

When you do connect with your new contacts, the most critical thing you can do is acknowledge them. Before you connect, the button beside the profile picture says, "Connect." After you connect, it says, "Send a message." When I connect with another person, one of the key things I do is click that button and send them a message thanking them for connecting with me. This is the best way to build relationships on LinkedIn and it takes just 60 seconds.

Group Etiquette & Settings

Did your grandma ever tell you to take your elbows off the table? How about which fork to use to eat the salad? And how many times have you been told not to talk with your mouth full? These are all forms of etiquette. Believe it or not, forms of etiquette exist in dealing with groups on LinkedIn as well. Many realtors will jump into just realtor groups. Job seekers do the same thing. They jump into every Job group they can find.

When a visitor looks at your profile and sees groups focused on job seekers, they think that if they reach out to you, all you will want from them is a job.

One time I was in a real estate office talking with a friend and another person walked in the door. All of a sudden 30 agents in the office picked up the phone.

I said to my friend, "What the heck was that? I just saw 90% of the agents grab the phone and stick it to their ear."

My friend laughed and said, "Yeah, that man who walked in is a title company representative. The agents put the phone to their ear so the title person wouldn't stop at their desk to talk to them. It is their way of avoiding telling him they are too busy to talk."

Social media is not about the exploitation of technology but service to community.
--Simon Mainwaring

The same thing can happen on LinkedIn. When you put the wrong group logos on your profile, many people will not want to connect with or talk to you. The best way to avoid this is to hide the group logos that aren't attractive to your viewers.

When you set up your group membership settings, make sure to unclick two items, your logo for the groups you don't want others to see and your digest, unless the group is one of your top three, in which case you want to get every message everybody is sending because this is your tribe. You don't want every message from the other 49 groups. Unclick the daily digest if you don't want to get daily or weekly messages. However, always click the bottom two buttons which allow the Group Manager to send you email and other members to send you messages.

For digest emails, you have a choice of weekly or daily emails. A very busy person will unclick both of those for all but a few groups. You can change the settings from a daily notice to a weekly notice if you prefer. For groups where there is too much chatter, don't allow digest messages.

Groups are like the Super Bowl 50

It seems almost unpatriotic not to watch the Super Bowl, so I turned on the game and thought, "No way" when I saw it was the big one, Number 50. Who hasn't watched a super bowl? It's the #1

American game of the year. To be ironic, Carlos Santana sang and played. It brought back a lot of memories.

We all want to win but it is how we play the game. In groups you must pick the ones you relate to, know it has the people you want to play with, and that it is the place you're willing to invest some time in. When you are post an article, you wrote or one you want to share, ask yourself, "Is there alignment my values and needs."

Diversify Your Groups

Entrepreneurs

Executives - Boomers - **Entrepreneurs** [Member]
Former CMC, Now...Executives-Boomers-**Entrepreneurs**! We focus to assist each other in developing lifetime relationships &...
1,147 members
Similar

On Startups - The Community For **Entrepreneurs**
Startup community for **entrepreneurs** and small business owners. If you're an entrepreneur, you should join the largest ...
543,337 members
Similar

Small Business Network: Startups & **Entrepreneurs** talk Social Media Marketing Startup Jobs Sales PR
Small Business Network is for the entrepreneur founder & owner. **Entrepreneurs** who startup grow SMB & SMEs. Discuss online ...
114,009 members
Similar

A Startup Specialists Group - Online Network for **Entrepreneurs** and Startups (Business Jobs Careers)
Venture Capital Investors Angels VC IT Digital Tech Finance Media Social Legal Mobile Pharma Biotech Cloud PR Legal in ...
205,555 members
Similar

Here are This Chapter's Business Consultant Influencers

As you read these profiles, look for possible referrals for your needs.

Is there something in their story you connect with?

Could you gain a new idea or insight for your business or career?

Who do you know or who do they know that can help both of you?

If you needed help or wanted to buy a product, what would it be?

How do you follow up when you meet someone?

When people view your profile, how do you want them to feel?

Do your tribes line up so you could be Power Partners?

What are your favorite questions to ask in an introductory call?

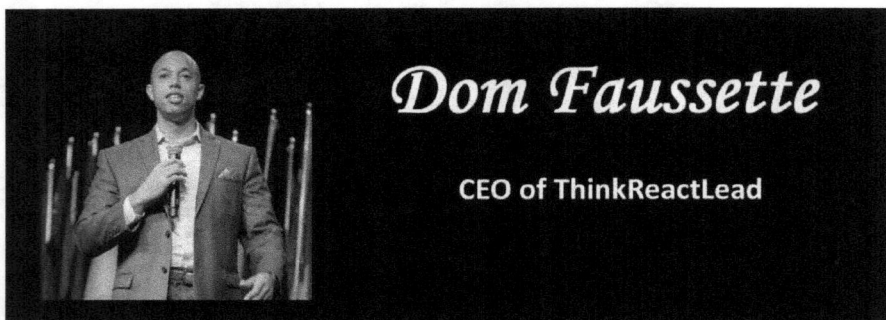

"Great leaders are almost always great simplifiers, who can cut through argument, debate and doubt, to offer a solution everybody can understand." - Colin Powell

As a child I was challenged by severe stuttering, and I was extremely quiet around others. It took until I was 21 and serving in the United States Air Force with the 305th SFS as a K9 handler to learn how to be comfortable in my own vulnerability when I developed a relationship and talked to my dog.

Later as a Police Officer with the City of Jackson, Mississippi I had to make a split-second decision on whether or not to take a perpetrators life during an altercation. I decided against it and resigned with two-weeks notice. In that moment of clarity, I realized that my purpose in life is to develop and encourage vulnerable leadership.

Today, I'm a certified speaker/coach with the John Maxwell Leadership Team and founder of my own company, Leaders 4 Leaders, LLC. I continue to work nationally with the best and brightest in the leadership development field.

▶ Tenured Executives with a desire to operate within their purpose
▶ C-Level Executives who have an unfulfilled passion
▶ Higher Educated Professionals with positions that aren't commensurate with their degree/s

Specialties: Leadership Speaking / Training and Facilitating / Motivational Speaking / Executive Coaching / Corporate Facilitator

Who in your childhood was a major influence that helped shape your life? The major influencer during my childhood was my mother, Lisa Faussette. She taught me the value of self-respect, hard work and belief in self no matter the circumstances.

If you could be anyone for a day, who would it be and what experience can you envision? If I could be anyone for a day, I'd be "ME", a decade from today. I envision speaking to an audience of thousands about the benefits of VULNERABILITY with my wife and children by my side.

What discipline could someone learn from you? The discipline someone can learn from me, would be learning how to have FUN! We must first understand that things and people will never bring us the happiness that we desire most. Once we bridge the gap between our mind and our heart, we can then move towards a life of FUN!

Dom's Favorite Characteristics
Grit, Determination, Forward Thinker, Passionate Speaker, Integral, Servant Leadership, service before self, relatable, good listener, compassionate

Dom Faussette aka *"Speaking Cadre"*
"CONNECT WITH YOUR AUTHENTIC PURPOSE.THINK. REACT. LEAD"
♛ Leadership Speaker ♛ Motivational Speaker ♛ Corporate Facilitator
♛ Executive Coach
♜ thinkreactlead@gmail.com ♟ 602-481-0650 ♛
www.thinkreactlead.com ✓

Ryan Matthews

2x TEDx Speaker
Author
Serial Entrepreneur

Ryan Matthews is an inspirational speaker, author and decorated veteran who trained elite Army K-9s and then became a civilian dog-trainer using his proven formula (RCTR) to train over 3,000 dogs. He earned almost $1,000,000 in 2½ years. Ryan is passionate about bridging the gap of communication between dogs and their owners. He does with World Of Dog Training.com (online dog training videos) and Peace Of Mind CBD.com, a natural health option for dogs with pain, mobility issues and behavioral problems.

Despite Ryan's overwhelming success building a dog-training empire, he felt like a failure. As a self-professed workaholic, Ryan put all his energy and focus into his work rather than into himself. After years battling childhood trauma and combat PTSD, the result was multiple life-threatening diagnoses and 5 near-death experiences. Through self-discovery, Ryan has transformed his life and has made it his mission to share his gifts and talents to positively transform the lives of others.

Author of The Canine Connection, Ryan is an inspirational speaker who talks about PTSD and transformation. His first TEDx talk is called "Overcoming PTSD with Dog Training Techniques," his second talk is "Treat People Like We Treat Dogs." He also has an upcoming book on his story of 5 near-death experiences and the transformation after a life filled with trauma. There is no better title for his journey other than "Survivor To Thriver!"

Ryan Matthews
www.WorldOfDogTraining.com
www.IAmRyanMatthews.com
www.PeaceOfMindHemp.com
linkedin.com/in/iamryanmatthews
Or call 844.448.DOGS (3647)
Social media:@IAmRyanMatthews

People are not remembered
by how few times they fail,

but by how often
they succeed.

Every Wrong Step
is another step forward.

Thomas Edison

Chapter 7
Follow-Up and Follow-Through

It's far greater to eliminate one weakness than to add one strength.
-- General Shigo, Last Samurai

Tom Muzila

Self Empowerment Speaker, Teacher
Special Forces Green Beret
Martial Arts Master

My Influencers: Tom Muzila

I went to an Investment meeting on the 10th floor of one of the buildings across the street from the Larry Flint building in Beverly Hills. My friend Barry Axelrod invited me to attend to meet investors who wanted to build a Veterans Community that included homes and activities like fishing & horseback riding and a six-week retreat to help Veterans heal for peace. At the meeting I met Tom Muzila.

Tom Muzila is a powerful teacher, lecturer, and speaker on self-empowerment. He is considered by various martial art magazines to be one of the top teachers and practitioners in the world. He has practiced and taught karate and martial arts for over 30 years. Tom has devoted his entire life to studying, researching and practicing optimum peak performance mental concepts and mind over matter type of accomplishments and feats.

Muzila is a 5th degree black belt in Shotokan Karate, but has practiced numerous other martial arts and boxed. He has participated on the U.S. Karate Team various times. He holds many karate athletic world records, which exhibit incredible physical, mental stamina and endurance. Some of these are practicing karate techniques for 24 hours straight. He has punched and kicked 10,000 times in one session on numerous occasions. He's gone through 100 Karate Special Trainings, which is more than anyone in the world. He has also accomplished a 21-day Karate Special Training, which encompassed training 9 hours a day for 21 days. He is also an expert with internal (Chi) energy.

In addition, Muzila served in the Special Forces, (Green Berets) in the military. He attended and graduated from some of the toughest military elite survival schools, such as: airborne, ranger, jungle warfare, mountaineering, light and heavy weapons, pathfinder, desert and cold weather survival, sniper, scuba, visual tracking, HALO and numerous others. He is one of the top combat instinct shooting instructors available.

Now, let's look at some other mental and physical feats he has done. He has climbed 6 mountains in 7 days. Tom has walked barefoot over red hot burning coals over 100 times, without being burnt or injured. He's squatted with an 8-pound iron ball 10,000 times, which took over 2 ½ hours. He's stood in a low karate horse stance for 3 hours. Tom has pulled 20,000-pound diesel trucks and an F-16 Air Force Fighter Jet. He has run 50 miles and 25 miles many times continuously.

If you don't want to get wet, jump in the lake.
--Master Oshima

He is also an expert in professional bodyguarding and has specialized in celebrity protection through the years. He has protected hundreds of the most famous celebrities in the world, such as: Warren Beatty, Steven Seagal, Bruce Willis and Sharon Stone. He's protected presidents, such as Clinton and Reagan.

He has also been in charge of security for huge benefits and events, where numerous celebrities and some of the most affluent and wealthiest individuals in the world have attended. In addition, he has taught numerous law enforcement agencies and elite military groups and units in various subjects. He has a degree in Asian Religions and has specialized in researching para-psychological techniques as applied to success and achievement.

He teaches classes in Karate-Martial Arts, Counterterrorist tactics and Close Quarter Combat skills.

Follow-up is a Winners Game

There can be a thousand excuses why a potential contact didn't follow up with you or you didn't follow up with a new acquaintance. Either way, when follow-up doesn't happen ask yourself how your potential contact might like to be followed up with, either by phone, text, or e-mail. If you don't know, find out!

Some people may get 200 emails a day, some people have an assistant who handles their emails and that gatekeeper may have already recycled you. Don't call a person during non-business hours if you are not a personal friend because you have no personal connection. On the other hand, if you're going to meet with them at a charity run on the weekend, an after-hours call may be appropriate. If you are calling someone on a Sunday and they have Sunday reserved as a family day, you lose relationship currency.

Texting is another tricky subject. One time I was doing a favor for some people by updating their profiles on LinkedIn. When I finished, I let them know that the profile was changed and asked them to go in and check it out. I didn't hear anything from them right away, so I went on with other things and figured we would catch up later. I didn't mean 3:30 a.m.! In the middle of the night, when I was fast asleep, my cell phone started squawking. OMG...who could be texting me at this horrible hour! It must be an emergency! Startled and confused, I got out of bed to check the message. What did I find? A text from one of the team members I was working with on the LinkedIn site, telling me about grammar mistakes and spelling errors. "Are you kidding me?" I thought. "It's 3:30 a.m. and they woke me up to tell me that?" I was not happy.

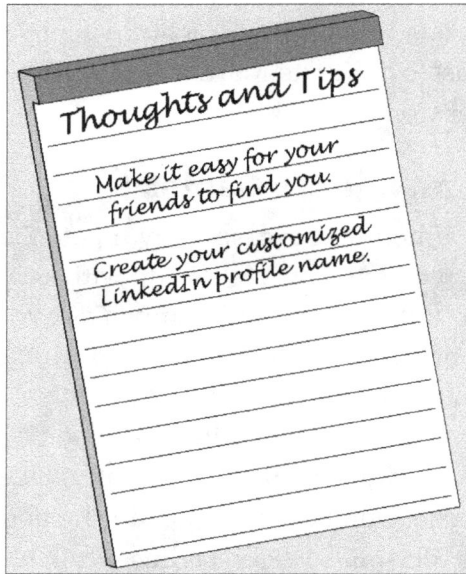

Thoughts and Tips

Make it easy for your friends to find you.

Create your customized LinkedIn profile name.

Remember, timing is everything. Be aware of what you're sending, when you're sending it, and how professional the content you're sending is. It can make a huge difference.

Another lesson I learned is that the bigger the person you want to contact, the more cautious and strategic you need to be in your follow-up. Asking them repeatedly for a connection or conversation will only tick them off. Once you make this mistake, you have created a negative relationship that could haunt you for years. Look at the big picture. If you are a screenwriter on a project that could take years, maybe your follow-up would be every other month. Base your follow-up timing on the players in your game of chess.

The best follow-up on LinkedIn is to send an invite. If they accept, send a thank you note and send your next step, which usually turns into a phone call opportunity. From the phone call, the next step is to meet in person. From there, take steps as the situation warrants. For instance, if you are in medical sales and you planned to meet a doctor to play a round of golf, consider the possible commission from that meeting and the possible referrals that doctor could give you to new doctors or hospitals that might use your company's products. What if that commission was worth $10,000? Ask yourself how you would approach that client. The answer is clear: Ask that client for an appointment and follow up with them. Treat them like gold. Most people miss these opportunities because they don't realize the potential of a simple first meeting. The first impression they make kills the future possibility.

Reach Out and Touch Someone

In sales we have a follow up system we call the "14 touch points." In some industries, sales representatives drop off a card and a Payday candy bar. It sounds silly and simple but consider this scenario. If it was 3 p.m. on a Friday afternoon and you loved Payday candy bars and you returned to the office to find a Payday sitting on your desk waiting for you, you would be very excited. When you notice that your sales representative delivered it because he remembered a conversation where you said you loved them, it leaves a positive feeling. You knew he was in a different city on Fridays and must have driven to your city just to drop of the candy bar before heading back to his office to turn in his required Friday reports. He just made himself your favorite rep and the next time you need to order his product you will remember him! That 50-cent candy bar might just have made him a nice commission.

Ask, Ask, Ask for Help and Referrals

The biggest challenge that is I see people have when they network is also one of the three biggest challenges people have in communication. This is true for everyone, male or female, young or old. They have great difficulty saying:

1. I love you
2. I'm sorry
3. Can you help me?

An ordinary person is ready for the expected, an extraordinary person is ready for the unexpected.
—Tom Muzila

We seem to forget our purpose when we are networking. For example, if you are looking for a job, after you have identified your contact and built a relationship, you must be clear when you request help and ask specifically what you are looking for. The key is to ask! If you want the person to introduce you to an important executive….ask! If you want to connect through LinkedIn to a CEO at a company you want to work for, ask for an introduction. Use your connections to your benefit. "Can you connect me with John Smith? He's the Vice President of Merchandising and I'm thinking about applying there in six months." Send two simple sentences to someone in your network who knows John Smith and who knows, you might just get an interview.

Be larger than your task.
—Orison Sweet Marden

Who are your Top Five Companies?

In networking, part of your pitch is to share what company you would like to work for. Even more important than your pitch is your follow-up. Make a list of five to seven different ways you can share your mission with people. Ask yourself why you want to work for them. Re-read the job description and find out what they are looking for. Tailor your follow-up specifically to what they want.

Companies

USA TODAY
Newspapers
✓ Following

American Marketing ...
Marketing and Advertising
✓ Following

Umpqua Bank
Banking
✓ Following

Verizon
Information Technology
and Services
✓ Following

Ocean Bank
Banking
✓ Following

AV Event Solutions
Events Services
✓ Following

Peak Potentials
Professional Training &
Coaching
✓ Following

National College Plan...
Education Management
✓ Following

Sears Home Services
Consumer Services
✓ Following

Boston Private Bank
Banking
✓ Following

Udemy
E-Learning
✓ Following

Chevron
Oil & Energy
✓ Following

Dell
Information Technology
and Services
✓ Following

Socal BNI
Professional Training &
Coaching
✓ Following

Dale Carnegie Training
Professional Training &
Coaching
✓ Following

HDFC Bank
Banking
✓ Following

Example:

Dear Mr. Brown,

I am in retiring from my current job in three months. I have started to identify possible part-time jobs and companies that interest me. In my search, I found your marketing position and would like to discuss the possibility of applying for this job before I retire. I want to thank you in advance for the opportunity and ask that if you know of anyone or any LinkedIn group that can help me on my path, please share my information with them and help me on my mission.

Thank you again for accepting my LinkedIn invite.
I hope to be an added contributor to many others in the future.

Signed by you
(Your current email address)
(Your current phone number)

Only one thing…a desire so strong, a determination so intense, that you cheerfully throw everything you have into the scale to win what you want. Not merely your work and your money and your thought, but the willingness to stand or fall by the result — to do or to die.
--Robert Collier

Identify the top five companies you want to work for. Research them and identify jobs within these organizations that interest you. Find the names of people in these organizations and see if they are on LinkedIn. If so, see if anyone you're connected to is connected to them. Search the actual companies on LinkedIn and see if they have a LinkedIn presence or have available jobs listed. Many companies use LinkedIn to list job opportunities. Find out everything you can about the five companies you have identified and become a top candidate for them.

Identify your Top 20 Connections

It was character that got us out of bed, commitment that moved us into action, and discipline that enabled us to follow through.
--Zig Ziglar

Have you ever met a person and later said to yourself, "I wish I had followed up or I should have stayed in touch with…" When I was in my 20s, a real estate broker said to me, "If you have 100 people who like you, know you and trust you, you won't be looking for a job or a friend."

As life passes, we see many changes along our path. Friends move, we move, we lose touch. One of my challenges was that after 30 years I hadn't kept in touch with many of my early contacts. I had missed many opportunities.

Marketing is not an event, but a process… It has a beginning, a middle, but never an end, for it is a process. You improve it, perfect it, change it, even pause it. But you never stop it completely.
–J. Conrad Levinson

There's a saying I like a lot: "You can save a lot of time (time is money) if you learn from someone else's mistake." LinkedIn makes it easy to stay in touch with people, even those you lost contact with long ago. In the section on connecting, I showed you a memory jogger that helps you rediscover people you met in your past and recent present.

Begin by making a list of people you have connected with at your various jobs. The memory jogger will also help when you do your CRM (Client Retention Management).

You can use this as you develop your 100 top people. Since you are new at developing your relationships, this list will shift based on how future relationships and alignments develop as you meet more people.

I believe that you can get everything in life you want if you will just help enough other people get what they want.
--Zig Ziglar

Here is the recipe for who could be good resources for job connections: Four recruiters, Four alumni, Four current employees, and Four people from groups.

President Reagan wrote Five Thank You notes a day

Ronald Reagan was the 40th President of the United States and was one of our oldest presidents. Prior to his presidency, he served as the 33rd Governor of California. When he ran for office a common comment was, "Is this a joke?" because he had been on radio, television and in movies. Could a celebrity really run the country?

Not only was President Reagan one of our favorite presidents, he also had a gift for connecting with people. His style was to make connections personal so that people never forgot him. One of his professional business habits was to write five thank-you notes every day.

We keep moving forward opening new doors and doing new things, because we're curious and curiosity keeps leading us down new paths.
--Walt Disney

On LinkedIn, writing a thank-you is a wonderful way to start your relationships with new connections. When you say "thank you" and acknowledge your new LinkedIn friend or future colleagues, you are well on your way to building a personal relationship with them.

Here are This Chapter's Business Consultant Influencers

As you read these profiles, look for possible referrals for your needs.

Is there something in their story you connect with?

Could you gain a new idea or insight for your business or career?

Who do you know or who do they know that can help both of you?

If you needed help or wanted to buy a product, what would it be?

How do you follow up when you meet someone?

When people view your profile, how do you want them to feel?

Do your tribes line up so you could be Power Partners?

What are your favorite questions to ask in an introductory call?

Eldonna Lewis Fernandez

Think Like a Negotiator

The power is in the work, you do the work you will have power to achieve your goals and dreams. ~ Eldonna Lewis Fernandez

I grew up as the daughter of 2 alcoholic parents. My mother died when I was 12 years old from alcoholism. I dropped out of High School and was heading down a loser's path. My faith in God, helped to create a "victory" mindset of not allowing failure to stand in the way of achieving greatness. Twenty-three years of military service produced a lifelong service mentality. Determination & tenacity helped me graduate with 2 associate degrees & a bachelor's degree in Contracts and Business Management.

For over 30 years, I've been a contract's negotiator and leader. In 2007 I became a keynote speaker, trainer & consultant. Today, I show people how to become more confident, competent & productive by improving their negotiation, leadership & communication skills in their daily work. I'm known for bringing an audience to life & helping them to get their "ask" in gear by thinking like a Negotiator & a Leader.

"Filled to capacity, standing room only, outstanding presentation. The Think Like A Negotiator session provided takeaways for attendees to hone their negotiation skills." R. Baranick, Deputy District Director U.S. SBA

Do you want Your Employees or Conference Attendees to have:

▶ Increased level of confidence?

▶ Ability to communicate with clarity and purpose?

▶ Understanding how to interact/negotiate with different personalities?

▶ Improved work environment where communication flows?

▶ Increased sales, productivity and bottom line?

Clients include Raytheon, Los Angeles Air Force Base, California Board of Equalization, California State University Fullerton, US Department of Veteran Affairs, Southern California Edison, Toastmasters International.

Certified Small Disadvantaged Veteran and Woman Owned Business

SPECIALTIES: Expert Negotiator & Contracts Manager, Internationally Accredited Speaker on Negotiation, Leadership & Communication, Sought After Motivational & Inspirational Speaker, Consultant & Trainer

1.   What 3 books do you feel are a must that you highly recommend to others. The Purpose Driven Life (Rick Warren), Mary Kay on People Management (Mary Kay Ash), Influence (Chaldini)

2.   What will you do differently this year from last year or what do you want more of? First I'll start with an "After Action Review" of the year focusing on what worked, what didn't and what I can improve on for next year. Then make course corrections, eliminate those things that didn't work or adjust them to produce a different result. Remove negative un-supporting & selfish people from my life.

3. **What discipline could someone learn from you?** Make your bed everyday – start the day disciplining yourself to complete a simple task which carries over into the bigger tasks.

4.   When "winning someone over" do you think facts or emotions carry the day? It depends on their archetype on how they receive information. Relationship capitol – building relationships and genuinely connecting with someone will "carry the day."

5. **What do you wish you spent more time doing? What prevents you from doing this now?** I wish I had more time to ride my Harley. My speaking travels have limited the time I get to ride. I am making a course correction to ensure that I get more riding time in the future.

6. **In helping others, is it better to teach them, give them or show them?**

Benjamin Franklin said Tell me and I forget, teach me and I may remember, involve me and I learn." Telling or giving someone something doesn't have as big of an impact as teaching and involving people in it. People learn by doing that is why the trainings I provide are experiential in nature. You can't learn negotiation by passively listening to it, you have to do it to get good at it. We do that in all our trainings.

7. If there were one problem in the world you could solve, what would it be? Hate and negativity. The media sensationalizes negative things and the more negative the better. People wouldn't say to someone's face the negative hateful comments many say online. Only love and kindness will eradicate negativity.

Eldonnas's Favorite Characteristics

Strategy, Discipline, Genuine Faith, Integrity, Optimism, Service-Minded, Tenacity, Determination, Negotiator, Communicator, Community
Service

Eldonna Lewis Fernandez aka #I Negotiate

"A speaker who brings your audience to life, leaving them impacted, inspired & educated, by learning how to ask for exactly what they want and get it. Trainer & Consultant to major corporations and Government agencies."

♛ Author ♛ Accomplished International Keynote Speaker and Trainer ♛ Proven Negotiator ♛ Negotiation, Leadership and Communication Skills that Drive Success

♟ eldonna@thinklikeanegotiator.com ♟ 310-591-9803 ♛
eldonnalewisfernandez.com basketsandbeadskenya.com

You cannot change the world,

But you can present the world with one improved person -- Yourself.

You can go to work on yourself to make yourself

Into the kind of person you admire and respect.

You can become a role model and set a standard for others.

You can control and discipline yourself to resist acting

Or speaking in a negative way

Toward anyone for any reason.

You can insist upon always doing things the loving way,

Rather than the hurtful way.

By doing these things each day,

You can continue on your journey

Toward becoming an exceptional human being.

Brian Tracy

Chapter 8
Recommendations, Marketing

Customer satisfaction is worthless. Customer loyalty is priceless.
--Jeff Gitomer

Isaac Belden

**CEO and Board President
Veteran Entrepreneur Alliance**

My Influencers: Isaac Belden

As you may know, I love *Think and Grow Rich*. One of its main principles is to use a Mastermind, where two or more persons brainstorm, sharing ideas and creating connections.

I've done masterminds in Beverly Hills, Newport Beach, Las Vegas and this time I went to Scottsdale to join my good friend Brandon Barnum, who had created a referral company. One of his guests was Isaac Belden.

I asked him what he did today.

"I launched a nonprofit organization called the Veteran Entrepreneur Alliance (VEA) after I served twelve years in the Idaho National Guard, including 18 months in Iraq beginning in 2004." The VEA is my passion. This organization was born from the belief that as veterans we lose two things when we leave service. The first is our sense of purpose. For many of us our identity is thoroughly entangled with our military service. When that time is over, we find ourselves wondering who we will be without it. The second is our sense of connection and community. The people and structure we grew accustomed to are suddenly gone and it's on us to find our way."

"Tell me about your service."

"A lot of Post 9/11 veterans have a story of bravery behind their choice to enlist. Many of them signed the dotted line because they saw what happened in New York and wanted to play a role in making sure nothing like that ever happened again. My story is different. I joined on March 13, 2001, six months prior to the towers being hit. I was a 17-year old kid with no idea what I wanted out of life. I just knew I didn't want to become my parents. My dad walked out when I was very young, and my mom treated my sister and I like punching bags from time to time. I didn't want to live the paycheck to paycheck lifestyle, I wanted to do more, and I believed that the military would help me find that. So, I convinced (tricked) my mom into signing a form for me to enter the military before my 18th birthday."

What was our experience like?"

"I served as a 12B (Combat Engineer) in the Idaho Army National Guard for 12 years. This is something that I carry with me as a point of pride. It would be safe to say that many of my years were spent as what some would call a "weekend warrior". But the effect of even those times created a profound change in my life. I learned to follow before learning to lead."

"What happened in Iraq?"

"In June 2004 I set out on an 18-month journey in support of Operation Iraqi Freedom. I served with the bravest men and women I have ever met. I fought with, against, and supported the Iraqi people in hopes that we could create real and lasting change. We did this not only to defend our country but to defend the Iraqi people who had no voice. It was this period of service that I describe as the best and the worst time of my life. This single experience has left scars both physical and mental that will never fully heal. It was also this experience that made me the man I am today and as I sit here today, I can honestly tell you that I am thankful to have had the opportunity to serve in that capacity."

Market like an Icon

Nike. Speedo. Coke. McDonald's. Nordstrom. Guess.

What do all of these names have in common? They're brands we recognize without any explanation. We know what they are, what they represent, and how to use them.

Developing your profile on LinkedIn is a form of branding. You're telling people who you are, what you represent, and how to use you in the future. Getting your brand across correctly is an important step. Finding the right words to communicate the right message is critical to your success.

Here's an example of branding from the banking business. Let's say someone has been successful in the home loan business. Now she wants to become a business developer, so she introduces herself this way, "Hi! My name is Nancy, I used to work for Bank of America doing home loans, but what I really want to do is to work with Chase as a business developer."

What is the one thing that people will remember about her? That she is in home loans. Don't tell people what you don't want them to remember. Craft your statement very carefully to remove what you don't want and emphasize what you do want, in this case a position with Chase. The same process applies to veterans and their military experience.

In your LinkedIn profile, tie the job description you want to everything in your profile. You may ask, "How do I make my future self into who I am now?"

It's not that hard, but it takes some thinking. You must ask the right questions to get the right answers. You tell people that you are seeking a position in whatever it is you want to do even though a lot of people say that you shouldn't do that. If you are looking for a position, you need to talk to people who know where the open positions are. You need to work on how you present your need. You may say that you "aspire for a position in...." which doesn't say you are a job seeker.

Furthermore, you need to remember that what you have done in the past has brought you to where you are today. List the places where you have volunteered and the places you have worked for. Be sure to include what you desire in all of your explanations. Tie your past into your future. This will brand you for what you want to become so people will think of you when they see the open position you are seeking.

What the mind of man can conceive and believe, the mind of man can achieve.
--Napoleon Hill

Credibility through Celebrity

Reality television shows are popular because they show how ordinary people can establish credibility through celebrity. It is a silent recommendation. If you are connected with celebrities, you must be a celebrity yourself. This is why you see so many celebrity product endorsements. It's tribal communication, meaning no words are exchanged. If a person you respect and admire likes a product or person, that product or person must be good. Why else would the celebrity endorse it?

The key point is that when you associate in any way with celebrities, you become more attractive to your peers and to potential employers. At first you may know only local celebrities. They may lead you to other even more influential celebrities like business leaders and former military officers, who can ease your way into the job market. Here are three examples of how persons who started out as non-celebrities used connections with celebrities become more credible and even become celebrities themselves. It's a great demonstration of credibility through celebrity.

Following

Influencers

Richard Branson
Founder at Virgin...
✓ Following

Jack Welch
Executive Chairman,...
✓ Following

Deepak Chopra MD (...
Founder, Chopra...
✓ Following

Bill Gates
Co-chair, Bill &...
✓ Following

Arianna Huffington
President and...
✓ Following

Jeff Weiner
CEO at LinkedIn
✓ Following

James Caan
Serial Entrepreneur...
✓ Following

Gretchen Rubin
Bestselling author;...
✓ Following

Anthony (Tony) Robbi...
Chairman at Anthony...
✓ Following

Tim Brown
CEO at IDEO
✓ Following

T. Boone Pickens
Founder, Chairman...
✓ Following

Daniel Goleman
Author of FOCUS:...
✓ Following

Guy Kawasaki
Advisor at Motorola...
✓ Following

Meg Whitman
CEO at...
✓ Following

Mark Cuban
President
✓ Following

Lou Adler
CEO, best-selling...
✓ Following

Twenty years ago, I met Jay Bennett, a home business coach and mentor and a trainer for multi-level marketers, through a network marketing company, Quorum, which was owned by Raymond Hung, one of the wealthiest entrepreneurs in Hong Kong. Jay worked in many Multi-Level Marketing companies, starting with Herbalife. Network Marketing companies have always attracted personal development and leadership people; and it's always been part of their coaching and training to get new distributors.

Jay taught me that it is easier to promote someone else than to promote yourself; just like it's easier to take photos of your friends than to shoot "selfies." If you have not yet made a million dollars, it makes no sense to promote yourself as a coach who can create millionaires. However, if you associate yourself with millionaires by getting yourself photographed with them, taking courses from them, or getting into masterminds with them, people will listen to you.

You will have many opportunities to meet and associate with millionaires. Celebrities tend to become role models for society. People accept what they see from celebrities, in many cases without verifying whether the information they hear is true or not. Having a celebrity brag about you and tell others how great you are will make your job search easier. If one of the people in your network is a celebrity and they decide to promote you, think of how much that helps you in your quest!

I shared in the chapter on networking a new connection who is not only my mentor but my friend. Another way to meet celebrities is through your friends who may be connected with celebrities. I've been to several dinner parties this new connection has hosted and met several celebrities there.

One of my favorite celebrities from those dinner parties is Glenn Morshower, best known for playing Secret Service Agent Aaron Pierce in 24. He has also been in *The Transformers* and *Grizzly Park*, always playing the colonel or the tough guy. It is fascinating to me that actors can shift easily into film roles even though in reality they are nothing like the characters they play. Glenn is the farthest thing from being a tough guy. He is a very funny man, with a memory like a fox.

He started out like everyone else, completely unknown. In his early days at auditions, he would go out for parts and not get them. He would study and work, but success eluded him. Then one day he put syrup in his shoes and he got the part. "Hmm," he thought, "Let's try something else." Next, he put cornflakes in his shoes and got the part. His wife was always part of his scheme and helped fill his shoes to insure he would get the part. Since his schemes were working, every time he auditioned he would create a ridiculous scheme to anchor himself. These games gave him the self-confidence he needed to start getting parts and build his own celebrity.

Luck is what happens when preparation meets opportunity.
--Seneca

One of today's most recognized seminar speakers is James Malinchak, famous for being on the *Secret Millionaire* television show. He trademarks himself as a Big Money speaker, and has created his *Big Money Speaker Boot Camp*, and his *College Speaker Success Boot Camp*. In both events, he develops and trains entrepreneurs to speak, coach, and build or improve their businesses. James is known for his philanthropic charitable gifts. In the *Secret Millionaire*, James helped three families get back on their feet with generous donations.

However, James was not always a celebrity. I remember him years ago speaking on small seminar stages to build his reputation. Unlike most of these speakers, James knew that to build celebrity, he needed to associate with celebrities. In the beginning, such opportunities were rare, but he took advantage of every one. It only takes a single connection to open the door and for James one connection led to many more.

Now he brings many celebrities he has met over the years to his events to share their message with the speakers and entrepreneurs in the audience.

One of my favorite celebrity speakers is Les Brown, whose events I've attended for over 20 years. He is often a guest speaker at Malinchak's events and the crowds love him. On the sports side, I enjoy hearing James' good friend Joe Theismann, a former National Football League quarterback. Theismann is the subject of several highly popular sports videos on YouTube showing the tragic, career-ending football injury he suffered in 1985. He teaches audiences that even after game changing events, you can turn your life into a huge success. James connects celebrities with his audiences and teaches them how to gain credibility by increasing their own celebrity connections. By using his celebrity connections, James Malinchak also gives his own event credibility.

You can give yourself credibility by finding and connecting with celebrities in the field you want to enter. They are not hard to find or meet if you position yourself correctly.

People Also Viewed

When you were a little kid did anyone ever tell you a fish story? My dad told me once we were going on a snipe hunt. We had to wait until the sun went down and it was dark. We had to be quiet and were searching for snipes with a flashlight. We put our shoes on grabbed our flashlights and pillowcases and headed out into the night to catch our snipes.

Lo and behold, my father had me outside calling for snipe but all I heard was a cricket. After 30 minutes my dad said there must not be any snipes out tonight and we came in. Later that summer he took me fishing. He gave me a fishing pole, taught me how to bait the hook and propped me up on a quaint little bridge. Then he tromped off in his golf shoes to shoot nine holes of golf. When he returned, I told him I had caught three fish. He shook his head. What happened was I did catch one fish but when I pulled him up and he hit the ground, a small fish popped out of this first fish and an even smaller fish came out.

Shared stories are bridge builders. This is one of my top 20 favorite functions on LinkedIn. On LinkedIn, when you as a viewer look at a person's profile, it shows you other people that that this person's viewers also viewed. For example, if you look up Oprah Winfrey, it may show you other talk show hosts that people also viewed. My favorite story of "Who knows Who" goes back to when I received an invite from the most successful real estate coach in the United States, CEO and real estate coach Mike Ferry™.

People Also Viewed

Oprah Winfrey · 3rd
CEO, Producer, Publisher, Actress and Innovator

Tim Ferriss · 2nd
Bestselling author, human guinea pig. Experiments: tim.blog

Jess Whitsen · 2nd
◆ Former Playboy Model Turned Successful CEO

Ashton Kutcher · 2nd
General Partner at Sound Ventures

Kevin Systrom · 3rd
CEO, Instagram

Kendall B. · 2nd
Product Marketing at Snapchat, Inc.

Zig Ziglar · 3rd
Founder at Ziglar Performance Group

Reed Hastings · 2nd
CEO Netflix

I looked at his profile, I noticed that people also viewed Floyd Wickman and when I clicked on Floyd I saw that people viewed Tommy Hopkins and when I viewed Tommy I saw people viewed Brian Tracy and when I clicked on Brian I saw that people viewed Tony Robbins and that put the biggest smile on my face because Tony was one of my mentors. :) When you use the "People Also Viewed" feature on LinkedIn, you identify people that you may not know but may need in your job search. Look at the "People Also Viewed" feature when doing research on LinkedIn and you may find some valuable connections.

Who knows Who

While viewing the profiles of potential recruiters, you may see something you like, maybe one of their second-level connections or someone who gave them a recommendation, someone they recommended, or maybe someone who endorsed them. You realize that you too want to connect with that person. When you click on that person's name or picture to look at their profile, it creates a path for spiders, the bits of software that track all LinkedIn activity. At the end of the day those paths are added up and you become part of the list of people who most viewed that person's profile. This is important because it is part of the social proof that begins with ripples, becomes rivers, and leads to tribes in this arena of online presence. Most of us are curious about who likes whom or who follows whom because in the job-searching world, that person may be the one who is one or two degrees or levels away from introducing us to our dream job. This applies to any activity, including hobbies, romance, and recreation.

Keep in Touch Marketing

In the Real Estate industry, a common practice is to send out a monthly newsletter. In other industries, companies send holiday postcards on special occasions every month, including Valentine's Day, Easter, St. Patrick's Day, Christmas, and Thanksgiving. All these cards include a special message advertising the company's service or specials.

Even the owner of a small business or a veteran starting out on a shoestring budget from his kitchen table can do this. This business owner will use Vistaprint to get his first set of business cards at a reasonable price. The next step for him is to print advertising postcards with photos of dogs wearing silly hats, cats dressed up in costumes, and even bearded dragons wearing dresses. Why? So he can make his business memorable.

This works on LinkedIn as well. Wouldn't it be cool if you updated your friends and family at the Holidays with not just a photo of your newest outfit but a real update? Share your events with "Photo Marketing" cards. Then, six months later, you can do even more updates. If you know the companies you're interested in working with, you can send the contacts from those companies your LinkedIn Profile.

Who did they recommend & who recommended them?

In the banking and loan business, a lender will ask for two years of tax returns or six months of previous utility bills to verify that payments were made in the manner necessary to grant the credit on a loan.

In the world of LinkedIn, when it comes to verifying a person's depth of experience, nothing speaks louder than recommendations from former colleagues and bosses. Using your network to build up strong recommendations is an important piece of the LinkedIn puzzle. When a potential employer sees a recommendation on your profile, it gives your resume extra validation and verification.

On the other hand, who have you recommended? Are you giving endorsements to the right individuals for the right reasons? When employers see who you have endorsed and recommended, they may also use this information in their decision-making process.

Brenda Cooper
Emmy Award Winning
Celebrity & Executive Image
Consultant / Fashion Stylist /
Color Expert & Keynote
Speaker
March 13, 2016, Brenda was a
client of Debra's

If you are looking to create an effective and impactful profile on LinkedIn your go to girl is Debra Faris. She is the ultimate LinkedIn Encyclopedia of everything there is to know to brand yourself online.
Debra is fun, unstoppable, inspirational and committed to you creating the life and career of your dreams. As a speaker and author I continue to enjoy every opportunity to learn, listen and

Josevie Jackson
Author ▪ Motivational
Speaker ▪ International
Personal Development
Coach ▪ Real Estate
Professional ▪
January 8, 2016, Josevie worked
with Debra but at different
companies

Debra Faris' LinkedIn training is phenomenal! She's full of information and tactics to help you build a better brand for yourself. Thank you, Debra for helping others take one step closer to achieving their success! :-)

Greg Loynd
No Fluff...just straight talk,
facts, and superior customer
service for Sellers, Buyers,
and Investors. 602.432.8123
January 8, 2016, Greg was a client
of Debra's

I was privileged to listen to an hour long interview & coaching session that Debra gave about LinkedIn strategies on 1/07/16 with Greg Hague of Real Estate Mavericks. Debra is an exceptional presenter. Her understanding of the inner workings of LinkedIn's capabilities and how to use them to boost a client's presence on the platform was truly amazing. I cannot wait to overhaul my profile using her strategies. Thank you Debra.

Jaylene Garrett
My Sellers NET More $$ ⌂
Proven Unique Selling
Formula ⌂ Featured in
FORBES ⌂ Your Real Estate
Goals are Priority ONE
January 19, 2016, Jaylene was a
client of Debra's

Debra is amazing! I love how she explains her linkedin system in easy step-by-step to-dos. I had NO idea how valuable my linkedin account was for building my business. I am a true believer and I appreciate the "abundance" she shares! Debra is the REAL thing!!

Testimonials are your best friend

The biggest question I get concerns my opinion on swapping recommendations. I admit that I didn't like the idea but when I thought about it, it seemed logical in certain situations.

Let's say I invested a lot of time coaching a client and gave them a tip that made them a very substantial amount of money and then realized that they had mentored me years before through a book they wrote that helped hundreds, thousands, or millions of people, including myself. I would want a recommendation from that person for the work I did and would not hesitate to give them one knowing the value of the services he had performed for me.

My answer to that question is simple. Was value exchanged? I won't write a general recommendation for you nor expect one from you if nothing of value happened. I would only recommend you if I personally experienced your value and can in good conscience stand behind the recommendation. Back in Chapter 1, "Who Am I," I showed you that if you were a Boy or Girl Scout and your scoutmaster had known you for years and knew your character well, they would stand behind their recommendation. The best recommendations come from people with the integrity to give an unequivocal positive recommendation.

Be a producer using iPhone Videos

For every force, there is a counter force, for every negative there is a positive, for every action there is a reaction. For every cause, there is an effect.
--Grace Speare

Have you ever used your cell phone to look up a YouTube video and then shared it with your friends because it meant something or was funny? By encouraging users to post videos and photos on the site, LinkedIn has made it easier for us to use technology to bring us to life for the world to see just like people on the big screen and on reality television. Make your profile more eye-catching by adding video. People love to watch movies, television, and YouTube. Let them watch a video of you!

LinkedIn has made it easier. Since we use our cell phones for everything now, including pictures and videos, we can make high quality visual presentations that make us all look professional on LinkedIn.

Here are This Chapter's Business Consultant Influencers

As you read these profiles, look for possible referrals for your needs.

Is there something in their story you connect with?

C9ould you gain a new idea or insight for your business or career?

Who do you know or who do they know that can help both of you?

If you needed help or wanted to buy a product, what would it be?

How do you follow up when you meet someone?

When people view your profile, how do you want them to feel?

Do your tribes line up so you could be Power Partners?

What are your favorite questions to ask in an introductory call?

Lisa Lockwood

Host, West Coast Weekly

Undercover Angel is the inspirational memoir of a woman who uses her beguiling femininity to take on the Mafia, infiltrate drug rings, and apprehend Internet child sex offenders. The edgy, often humorous narrative describes how Lisa Lockwood overcame the obstacles of her poverty-stricken childhood to become a Miss Illinois-USA contestant, a U.S. Air Force Desert Storm veteran, the first (and only) female member of a S.W.A.T team, and a highly decorated Narcotics and Undercover Detective in Chicago.

Lisa Lockwood is a highly sought-after media contributor, known throughout America for her insights on Crime in America as well as Career Reinvention for over a decade.

Known as the Reinvention Expert, Lisa is a decorated Desert Storm Veteran, Detective, SWAT Cop as well as career consultant, media personality, public speaker and Collegiate Educator.

She is an acclaimed author of the books:

"Undercover Angel: From Beauty Queen to SWAT Team"

"Reinventing YOU: The 10 Best Ways to Launch Your Dream Career"

"Heart of a Military Woman" (Co-Author)

1. What three books do you feel are a must that you highly recommend others to read? The Bible, The Secret, Think & Grow Rich

2. What movie touched you by its meaning or inspired you? Yentyl. When I watched the perseverance of the Yentyl character in the film, it resonated with me. The lengths the character went in her desire to study religion was met with great personal sacrifices. She needed to be someone else--a man, in order to pursue her life gal.

3. Who now is a Mentor, Coach or Strategist that is on your advisory council? My Christian faith, Joel Osteen and the teachings of Anthony Robbins.

4. If you could be anyone for a day, who would it be and what experience can you envision? If I could be anybody for a day, I would choose Jesus. I would love to experience what it was like when Jesus healed people who were blind or maimed.

5. What discipline could someone learn from you? Emotional Mastery. I've worked for years to learn how to reframe events in my life so as not to get caught up in drama, sadness, anger and misery. So when an event happens in my life my default is to ask the question "what could be great about this event happening to me?" Then I answer that question over and over again.

6. On what topic at parties would you really like to "get into it"? My favorite party ice-breaker has been asking people not what they do for a living but instead inquiring what it is they do for fun. They're usually shocked by the query and and soon begin to laugh or smile when reliving something fun they do in their lives.

7. If there were one problem in the world you could solve, what would it be? If I could solve one problem I would like to offer that people spend more time to Seek to Understand before judgement. With this alone we'd be a bully free society and more empathic toward our fellow man/woman. Thus my favorite quote. "Do Unto others as you have done unto you."

The nation that makes a great distinction between its scholars and its warriors will have its thinking done by cowards and its fighting done by fools.

Thucydides

Chapter 9
Jobs, Industries, and Culture

The willingness with which our young people are likely to serve in any war, no matter how justified, shall be directly proportional as to how they perceive the veterans of earlier wars were treated and appreciated by their nation.
--George Washington

Jesse Medina

Founder & President, Veteran Strong
NAB Veteran Hiring Support Liaison

My Influencers: Jesse Medina

Sometimes you can't help but believe that someone upstairs put you together. A good friend of mine, Lori Bohen, introduced me to Jesse Medina, who was a volunteer. Lori has been on the board of VIDC Veterans Independence Day, which is a 501c3 organization located right here in our backyard, Long Beach, California, that goes to the VA Hospital for the 4th of July. They serve over 3,000 Veterans and their families.

When I asked Jesse why he joined the service, he said he wanted to do something in life that had meaning, besides he came from a family that was "Veteran Strong", His grandfather and his chute were Army making him a third generation Army vet. His aunt was in the Marines and his nephew the Air Force.

"What happened to the Coast Guard?" I asked

He laughed. "Just a lot of friends."

"Tell me about the Golden Knights, the US Army Parachute Team." I said. "I did skydive once."

"There's a lot of jumps in 38 years."

"Any idea how many? 1,000's

Jesse developed a Global Virtual Veterans Enterprise Recruiting Platform that will be one of the biggest resources for our service members to align their Transition Advancement Procedure Redesigned (TAP-r2) from service to civilian. Creating an exit strategy is vital not only for our service members but also for our biggest Fortune 500 companies, who need experienced veterans to serve as strategic executives and to run the day-to-day duties for efficiency, profits & sustainability in America and in our companies that service international areas.

His non-profit organization, VeteranStrong-Non-Profit delivers products and services to support its mission of Training, Reintegration, Employment, Education, Entrepreneur, Healthcare and Housing (TREE H^2).

His for-profit company, VeteranStrong Career Resource Centers, develops and supports the Non-Profit's 501 (C)(3)'s Mission requirements, I.T., platforms and much more supported by HR.com our major installation provider.

When choosing between two similar applicants, hiring managers are increasingly turning to social media outlets to supplement information they are unable to glean from applications or interviews.
--Amy Jo Martin

Jesse Medina, CEO / President of VeteranStrong invited me to the 2nd RDAC meeting at Dodger Stadium, to induct Hall of Fame Manager Mr.Tommy Lasorda as his Honorary Co-Chair. This was a special event with 150 military and civilian personnel to include a traditional color guard ceremony. Jesse being the Chair for Navy Command Recruiting District Assistance Council (RDAC) and a

Army Recruiting member. Interesting fact that very few people know that at 18, Lasorda signed with the Philadelphia Phillies when he was drafted into the US Army and served two years at the end of World War II.

You are more than your resume

Names, dates, employers, job description. Is this how you want someone to judge you as a person? You are much than your resume. Do you manage others? Are you involved in execution, project management, or time management? Are you involved in charities? Do you have personal hobbies that you enjoy? You are more than a two-dimensional piece of paper with your work history listed on it. In many cases, potential employers use your resume to make decisions on who gets the interview and who gets the job. If you show up as a well-rounded person with interests and passions outside work, you are much more likely to get in the door.

Talent alone won't make you a success. Neither will being in the right place at the right time, unless you are ready. The most important question is: "Are you ready?"
--Johnny Carson

As you use LinkedIn and continue your career and personal thread, as we started to do in the "Who am I" chapter, you realize you are so much more than your resume. The most important question becomes, "How do you match yourself with your new LinkedIn friends from all areas of your life?" Building an effective profile, making strong connections, and connecting with the right influencers can give people much more insight into who *you* are as a person, both at work and at home. As more and more recruiters and employers use LinkedIn for recruiting purposes, a good profile will put you light years ahead of potential employees who include only work-related information on their profile.

The Difference Between Recruiters, Headhunters & Outplacements

Recruiters, headhunters, and human resources directors are all very important people to you in your quest for the right job. How do you find them on LinkedIn? Start with a LinkedIn search for people who use these titles in their descriptions. You will quickly identify the appropriate people for your industry. Connect with them and begin to develop a relationship with them. Connect to as many as you want. Then start to build rapport, find out what they're looking for in the perfect candidate, and examine their profile. Do your research, build a great relationship, and set yourself up for the perfect job.

Many groups on LinkedIn, if used effectively, can be instrumental in helping you find and land your dream job. Search and connect to groups in your chosen industry and then connect to the people in those groups. These connections will become extremely valuable as you look for interviews, recommendations, and networking.

Here's a bonus. I'm sharing my recruiter list of super-connectors with you. Each of these recruiters is connected to thousands of employers and can assist you in connecting the right employer for your field.

Top 12 Big Connectors - Recruiters & HR

Stacy (Berman) Birnbach | 25,000+ connections   1st
CEO/President Verus
Washington D.C. Metro Area | Staffing and Recruiting

Current: The Leukemia & Lymphoma Society, Verus Consulting Solutions, Verus Staffing Solutions
Previous: Health Search International and Clinical Resources, Health Search International, Clinical Resources Inc.
Education: University of Maryland

Send a message   Endorse ▼   500+ connections

Patrick Campbell
1st

Talent Acquisition Consultant at Public Storage

Greater Los Angeles Area | Staffing and Recruiting

Current   Public Storage
Previous   Union Bank [through Collabrus], TIAA-CREF through Pride Staffing, Campbell Executive Services, Inc.
Education   Ferris State University

Send a message   Endorse ▾

500+
connections

Derrick Coshow ★ Top Linked™ 21,000+
1st

Lead Technical Recruiter at Accolo

Las Vegas, Nevada Area | Staffing and Recruiting

Previous   Aristocrat, Link Technologies, Caesars Entertainment Corporation
Education   University of Nevada-Las Vegas

Send a message   Endorse ▾

500+
connections

Eric Grenier
2nd

30,104+ direct connections "Top 10 Most Connected" follow me on twitter: @comcentric

Greater Denver Area | Information Technology and Services

Current   Comcentric Inc.
Previous   RSA Companies, Profitool Inc., MW Builders / MMC Corporation
Education   University of Colorado at Denver

Connect   Send Eric InMail ▾

500+
connections

Bill Gunn
1st

G&A Principal | Build Your Talent Brand | Select the Exceptional from the Best | 23,315 Direct Connections Top 1% Viewed

Charlotte, North Carolina Area | Management Consulting

Current   G&A
Previous   Unisys, CSC, Mitsui & Co., Ltd.
Education   Old Dominion University

Send a message   Endorse ▾

500+
connections

Varsha Karnad - linkedin.varsha@gmail.com -Netwrk-22000+

1st

Executive – Human Resources at Kraft Foods

Mumbai Area, India | Human Resources

Current   Kraft Foods - Cadbury India Ltd
Previous   Indira School Of Business Studies, ISBS - Pune, Think People Solutions Pvt Ltd
Education   Indira School Of Business Studies - ISBS

Send a message   Endorse ▼   500+ connections

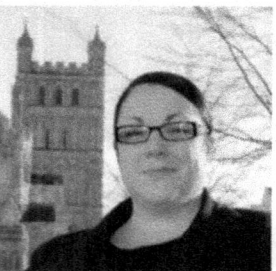

Ann Zaslow-Rethaber

1st

President at International Search Consultants AIRS Diversity Certified Recruiter

Phoenix, Arizona Area | Staffing and Recruiting

Current   International Search Consultants, Inc.
Previous   Owigi Films
Education   AIRS Diversity Certified Recruiter

Send a message   Endorse ▼   500+ connections

Pete Tzavalas 1,000+(LION)

1st

Sr. Vice President at Challenger, Gray & Christmas, Inc.

petetzavalas@challengergray.com 818.536.1415

Greater Los Angeles Area | Human Resources

Current   Challenger, Gray & Christmas, Inc.
Previous   Robert Half International, Right Management, Brinks Home Security
Education   Biola University

Send a message   Endorse ▼   500+ connections

Leonie Sands Mrep CertRP {LION 20,000+}

1st

Recruitment Consultant at Aptus Life Science

Exeter, United Kingdom | Staffing and Recruiting

Previous   Spinnaker Contract Services Limited, The Hammond Recruitment Group Ltd, Storm Recruitment
Education   University of Westminster

Send a message   Endorse ▼   500+ connections

Scott Simon   1st

BetterHire Provider/Consultant 29.999 connections

Birmingham, Alabama Area | Staffing and Recruiting

Current   Betterhire.com Provider/Consulting, TechnologyAlabama.com, Access Points

Previous   Adatech Inc., National Life, National Life Group

Education   University of Alabama at Birmingham

Send a message   Endorse ▼   **500+** connections

Phil Rosenberg   1st

LinkedIn's most connected Career Coach (30K+ 31M+), Author http://reCareered.com, Top 20 on Linkedin globally

Greater Denver Area | Human Resources

Current   reCareered, Business Week, PersonalBranding Blog, TheLadders, CIO, Fast Company, Career Central group on Linkedin

Previous   Robert Half Management Resources, Robert Half Technology, New Horizons Computer Learning Centers

Education   Northwestern University - Kellogg School of Management

Send a message   Endorse ▼   **500+** connections

Tom Toole   1st

One of the Management Recruiter's Most Connected Recruiters bringing "Midwest Work Ethic" to his Clients. 20k+ 1st LION

Orange County, California Area | Staffing and Recruiting

Current   Management Recruiters International/MRINetwork, Management Recruiter's International - Southern Ca.- National Market

Previous   The Coca-Cola Company, Wisconsin Air National Guard(USAF)-128th ARW, Caterpillar

Education   Marquette University

Send a message   Endorse ▼   **500+** connections

Websites are Your Research Tool

When you're interested in working for a company, you need to do your homework and research the company. Ask yourself why you would want to work for them. Take another look at the job description, review their website, and look for current events on the web. A job description tells you not just about the position you want but also gives you the voice of the company. See if their values align with yours. Check into their history, their ideals, their expectations, and investigate everything you can about the company and its hiring manager.

You can also connect with company insiders to get a sense of the corporate culture. If you are researching a public company, you can check quarterly and annual financial reports to get a feel for the challenges the company faces and the direction it is going.

No occupation is so delightful to me as the culture of the earth, and no culture comparable to that of the garden.
--Thomas Jefferson

Create a file for that company and add all the material that you find. Put the link to the company website in your file, create a list of key job titles, find the incumbents by searching on LinkedIn, add them to the list, review their profiles and invite them to connect. Your knowledge of your potential employer will make your interview more effective and will better equip you to understand whether the job fits your potential new career. Think of it as buying a textbook, highlighting the important lessons, identifying the takeaways, and using what you learned.

Positions vs. Industries

Are you searching for a position or do you want to be part of the industry? Using LinkedIn and managing your connections correctly can set you up for either. If you want to work in a certain industry, connect with successful people in that industry and influencers who reflect the industry, and then network with people currently working in the industry. If you seek a position, highlight your skills, connect with leaders and mentors who can assist you in achieving your goals, and gain the recommendations needed from leaders in your field.

Let's look at a few specific industries to give you a better idea. In the banking industry, for instance, the following might come to mind when you think of banking: branch manager, teller, loan officer, commercial banking, investment banking, financial services and management, the list is endless. You can investigate, research, and entertain hundreds of positions within the banking industry. Once you identify your ideal banking position, highlight your skills, and connect to the right team.

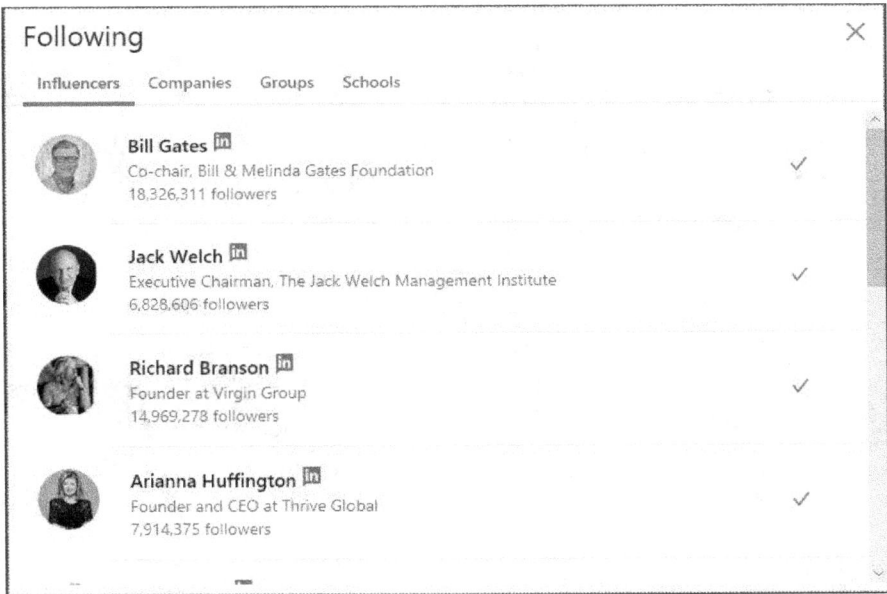

Following   ✕

Influencers   Companies   Groups   Schools

Bill Gates in
Co-chair, Bill & Melinda Gates Foundation
18,326,311 followers   ✓

Jack Welch in
Executive Chairman, The Jack Welch Management Institute
6,828,606 followers   ✓

Richard Branson in
Founder at Virgin Group
14,969,278 followers   ✓

Arianna Huffington in
Founder and CEO at Thrive Global
7,914,375 followers   ✓

Another avenue for many is the retail industry, which is always looking for great candidates. If you don't want to work in sales, look at the corporate part of retail, including buyers, operations managers, human resources, regional managers, training departments, again the list of opportunities is endless. Search by the position you seek and begin to interact with the people who can help get you there.

The entertainment industry is also huge. Are you a performer looking to be on movie screens in front of millions of fans, a singer with fans following your concerts across the country, or do you want to act on the Broadway stage? If performing does not interest you but you want to work in the entertainment industry, you can become a director, key grip, special effects person, design costumes, be a makeup artist, or become an executive assistant, screenwriter, caterer, or one of the many thousands of people that support the team on stage. Find the industry and position you want, and then use your connections on LinkedIn to build the relationships needed to get that job.

Culture is the process by which a person becomes all that they were created capable of being.
--Thomas Carlyle

To go deeper, if you see yourself as a leader climbing the corporate ladder, you may wonder, "How can I find that path?" Success does leave a trail and with LinkedIn you can see how mentors carve a path you can follow.

LinkedIn gives you the opportunity to see other people's success trails. On a CFO'S profile, you can see how he ended up in his current position by following his story on LinkedIn back 10, 12, or 15 years to where he or she started, perhaps as an accountant, then as a Certified Public Accountant (CPA) then controller and finally Chief Financial Officer (CFO).

Think International

Are you fluent in Spanish, Italian, Farsi, Cantonese, or German? Is your primary language something other than English? Back when I was in the loan business, I led a mastermind group for a Keller Williams Real Estate office. Acquiring new business was a key challenge. I asked a group of 10 real estate agents I knew, four of whom were Hispanic, three Chinese, one Cantonese, one Persian and one Polish, "Were any of you actually born in another country?" Half of them were. Then I asked, "Do you have family in another country?" Most of them had relatives overseas. I asked them whether there were any commonalities in their last names. The girl from

Poland said, "Yes, Polish names end in 'ski.'" I asked the title company if they could do a search by origin of names and they said yes. We began to hunt.

International Groups on LinkedIn

Organization	Members
Amnesty Intl (protect Human rights worldwide)	30,000
ASIS International	59,000
BNI - Business Network International	33,000
Builders, Owners, & managers International	43,300
IFMA International Facility Management Association	28,000
IIBA International Institute of Business Analysis	60,000
International Assn of Business communicators	32,000
International baccalaureate	25,000
International Business	71,000
International Coast Fed (Sustainable Development)	40,000
International Council of Shopping Centers	39,000
International Freight	28,000
International Import/Export	129,000
International Network for the Arts (Theater and art)	23,000
International Relations Professionals	30,000
International relations/Affairs	30,000
International School Educators	21,000
International Society for Technology/Education	41,000
International sports	27,000
International Trade	56,000
International TV Professionals	57,000
Jobs in NGOS	27,000
Sustainable Green	30,000
Technical Assistance Consultancy Network	34,000
Toastmasters International	36,000
Zezex (International Development)	47,000

If you know 100 people who know you, like you, and trust you, you have all the connections you need. This is especially true if you speak a foreign language. A former colleague, a bank branch manager, who spoke Farsi and had the biggest book of business in Orange County, put this idea to use when she advertised for business in Los Angeles. She attracted half her clientele from Los Angeles because many of them were more comfortable speaking their native language when they did business.

One of the challenges for any retail organization is communicating with people from different backgrounds. Another friend of mine managed a home improvement store in Los Angeles located in an area where Chinese-speaking individuals lived. Very few of them shopped at his store. To change that pattern, my friend found an employee who spoke Chinese and assigned him the mission of getting his Chinese friends to shop at the store. As an added inducement, he was to be their personal shopper, so they would feel comfortable when they arrived. The associate she picked was a special needs employee with a job coach. When his manager put him on his new task as Chinese Lead Generator, his eyes lit up and he was excited every time a new customer came to him for help. He became a needed individual in the store and was called on by all departments to assist in translation. It changed the way he looked at his job when he became a valued member of the team. Sales increased as more and more Chinese-speaking customers visited the store.

If you go on LinkedIn and put the word "Spanish" in the search engine and select "people," you will find over 4,546,000 names.

Polish people add 257,757, Chinese account for 1,115,000, and Italians 1,195,000. Continue your search in your native language or secondary language and you'll find thousands of individuals who share that language with you. Be sure to add all the languages you speak and your proficiency to your profile so those searching for speakers of other languages can find you easily.

EXECUTIVE TEAM | VP REPORTS TO JOBS | VICE PRESIDENT

JOHN BRANDON VP. CHANNEL SALES

MICHAEL FENGER VP. IPHONE SALES

DOUGLAS BECK VP. APPLE JAPAN

JOHN COUCH VP. EDUCATION SALES

JENNIFER BAILEY VP. ONLINE STORES

MICHAEL CULBERT VP. ARCHITECTURE

WILLIAM FREDERICK VP. FULFILLMENT

STEVE ZADESKY VP. IPHONE/IPOD DESIGN

KATIE COTTON VP. COMMUNICATIONS

JOEL PODOLNY VP. HR

RITA LANE VP. OPERATIONS

DAVID TUPMAN VP. HARDWARE ENGINEERING, IPHONE/IPOD

TIMOTHY COOK CHIEF OPERATING OFFICER

SABIH KHAN VP. OPERATIONS

BOB MANSFIELD SVP. MAC HARDWARE ENGINEERING

JEFFREY WILLIAMS SVP. OPERATIONS

DAN RICCIO VP. IPAD

DEIRDRE O'BRIEN VP. OPERATIONS

JOHN THERIAULT VP. GLOBAL SECURITY

BRUCE SEWELL SVP. GENERAL COUNSEL

JONATHAN IVE SVP. INDUSTRIAL DESIGN

JERRY MCDOUGAL VP. RETAIL

STEVE JOBS CEO

BETSY RAFAEL VP. CONTROLLER

PETER OPPENHEIMER SVP. CHIEF FINANCIAL OFFICER

RONALD JOHNSON* SVP. RETAIL

GREG GILLEY VP. VIDEO APPS

GARY WIPFLER VP. TREASURER

ANDY MILLER VP. MOBILE ADVERTISING/IAD

ROGER ROSNER VP. PRODUCTIVITY APPS

HIROKI ASAI VP. CREATIVE DIRECTOR

GREG JOSWIAK VP. IPHONE MARKETING

PHILIP SCHILLER SVP. MARKETING

SCOTT FORSTALL SVP. IOS SOFTWARE

HENRI LAMIRAUX VP. ENGINEERING, IOS APPS

MICHAEL TCHAO VP. IPAD MARKETING

CRAIG FEDERIGHI VP. MAC SOFTWARE ENGINEERING

EDDY CUE VP. INTERNET SERVICES

ISABEL GE MAHE VP. IOS WIRELESS SOFTWARE

DAVID MOODY VP. MAC MARKETING

KIM VORRATH VP. PROGRAM MANAGEMENT

RON OKAMOTO VP. DEVELOPER RELATIONS

JEFF ROBBIN VP. CONSUMER APPS

BRIAN CROLL VP. MAC SOFTWARE MARKETING

BUD TRIBBLE VP. SOFTWARE TECHNOLOGY

SIMON PATIENCE VP. CORE OS

MAX PALEY VP. AUDIO/VIDEO

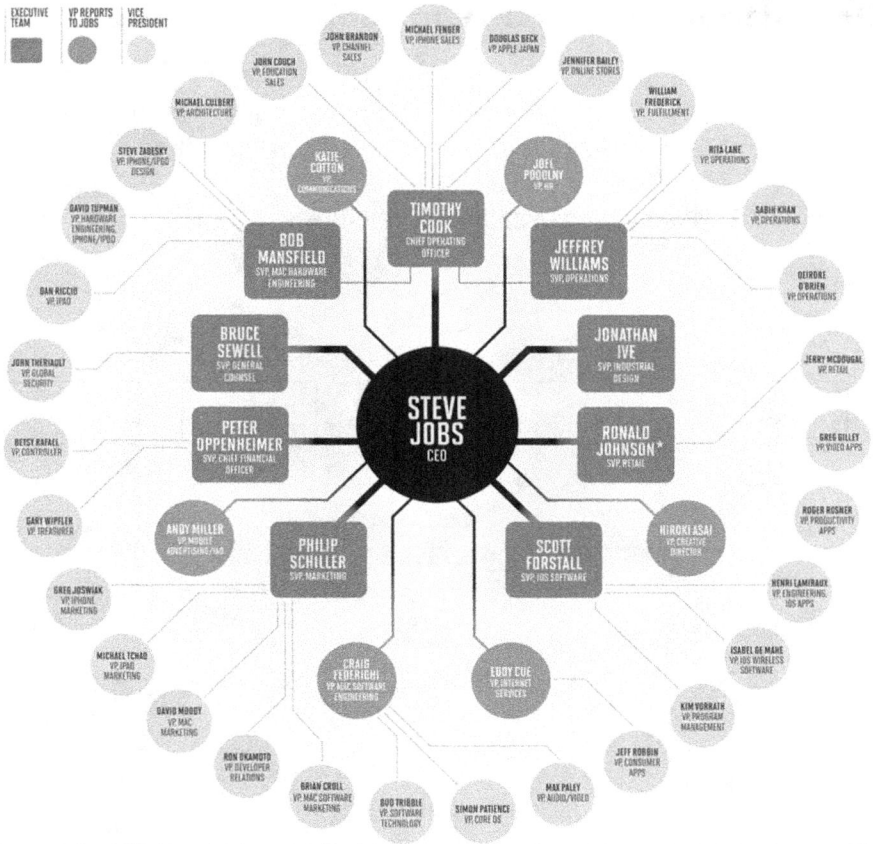

If you search the word "International" on LinkedIn, you will find 19,000 results. From financial services, IT, accounting, computer software, to management consultants, people around the world are connecting to each other. You will find 46,000 international groups on LinkedIn including fashion, import and export trade, freight, television professionals, veterans' groups, Beta Gamma Sigma honor society, and Toastmasters International. LinkedIn makes doing business on a global level easier.

The chart above shows you how many members many of the international groups on LinkedIn have.

Organizational chart: Who connects to who?

When researching a new company, one of the best things to use, if you can get it, is their organizational chart. This will show you how the company is organized and who is connected and how.

Sample Divisional Organizational Structure

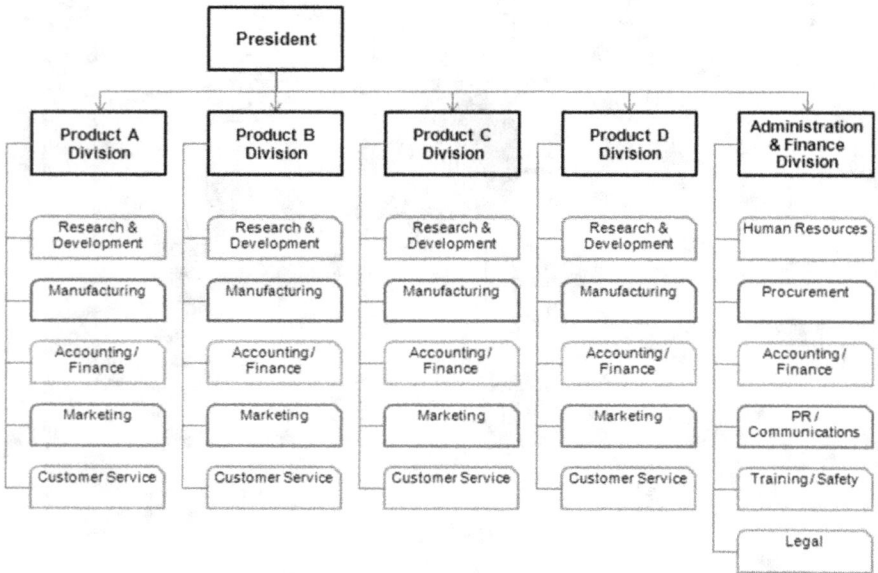

President				
Product A Division	Product B Division	Product C Division	Product D Division	Administration & Finance Division
Research & Development	Research & Development	Research & Development	Research & Development	Human Resources
Manufacturing	Manufacturing	Manufacturing	Manufacturing	Procurement
Accounting/ Finance	Accounting/ Finance	Accounting/ Finance	Accounting/ Finance	Accounting/ Finance
Marketing	Marketing	Marketing	Marketing	PR / Communications
Customer Service	Customer Service	Customer Service	Customer Service	Training/ Safety
				Legal

I am convinced that nothing we do is more important than hiring and developing people. At the end of the day you bet on people, not on strategies.
--Larry Bossidy

People Don't Hire Resumes, They Hire People

Whether he or she is CEO of the company or Director of HR, the hiring manager will always choose the best fit for the culture of their organization. In a research company, this could mean the best person is one who knows how to research in a creative way. In a sales position, they're looking for a relationship builder, an ambassador position, for a person with credibility. They hire you because of your character, your values, and your integrity. They hire you as a person.

| Jobs ▼ | Date Posted ▼ | LinkedIn Features ▼ | Comp |

Showing 19,184 results   Sort by: Relevance ▼   ⬚ Split View ▼

🔔 **Create search alert**

RICOH
adapts change

Business Process Services Sales Consultant - Lease Administration
Ricoh USA, Inc.
Greater Los Angeles Area
Primary responsibilities include, but are not limited to: prospecting, forecasting, lead management, coordinating, and implementin...

👤 1 connection works here

2 weeks ago · 🔗 Easy Apply

Cognizant

Business Analyst / Project Manager
Cognizant
Los Angeles, CA, US
Our Cognizant Veterans Network assists Veterans in building and growing a career at Cognizant that a... careers.cognizant.com

👥 3 connections work here

1 week ago

Union
Square

Digital Media Coordinator
Union Square Media Group
Los Angeles, California, United States
The Digital Media Coordinator will work hand in hand with our sales and account management team to provide campaign analytics and ...

2 weeks ago · 🔗 Easy Apply

How do you effectively align yourself or find the right people that will introduce you to the right people? Here's where using LinkedIn in an effective manner can be of great benefit! Once your profile is built with authenticity and transparency, you've started building relationships and connections with your top 100 as well as their top

100's, and you've done your research on your top five companies, it will all fall into place. You will be aligned with the right people. They will know your character and potential because of the relationship you have built with them. As you research the companies and people within those companies, your network will assist you in making the connections and aligning yourself.

Working for Non-Profits

After a conversation with Jim Palmer one day, I looked on LinkedIn and discovered that over 6,000 people had Non-Profit in their profile. While looking for opportunities, do not neglect non-profit organizations. These organizations represent amazing causes and hire people with all sorts of knowledge.

Find Connections in Your Top Five Companies

If you have created your profile on LinkedIn and have done your research as I've shown you, you will be well on your way to finding that new job. As you look at companies and opportunities, begin to identify the most important people in the companies you're searching.

Industry List from LinkedIn	
Accounting	Airlines/Aviation
Alternative Dispute Resolution	Alternative Medicine
Animation	Apparel & Fashion
Architecture & Planning	Arts & Crafts
Automotive	Aviation & Aerospace
Banking	Biotechnology
Broadcast Media	Building Materials
Business Supplies, Equipment	Capital Markets
Chemicals	Civic & Social Organization
Civil Engineering	Commercial Real Estate
Computer & Network Security	Computer Games

Computer Hardware	Computer Software
Construction	Consumer Electronics
Consumer Goods	Consumer Services
Cosmetics	Dairy
Defense & Space	Design
Education Management	E-Learning
Electronic Manufacturing	Entertainment
Environmental Services	Event Services
Executive Offices	Facilities Services
Farming	Financial Services
Fine Art	Fisheries
Food & Beverages	Food Production
Fund-Raising	Furniture
Gambling & Casinos	Glass, Ceramics, & Concrete
Government Administration	Government Relations
Graphic Design	Health, Wellness & Fitness
Higher Education	Hospital & Health Care
Hospitality	Human Resources
Import & Export	Individual & Family Services
Industrial Automation	Information Services
International Affairs	Insurance
Information Technology and Services	International Trade & Development
Internet	Investment Banking
Investment Management	Judiciary
Law Enforcement	Law Practice
Legal Services	Legislative Office
Leisure, Travel, & Tourism	Libraries
Logistics & Supply Chain	Luxury Goods & Jewelry
Machinery	Management Consulting
Maritime	Marketing and Advertising
Market Research	Mechanical Engineering
Media Production	Medical Devices
Medical Practice	Mental Health Care
Military	Mining & Metals
Motion Pictures & Films	Museums & Institutions

Music	Nanotechnology
Newspapers	Nonprofit Organization Mgmt
Oil & Energy	Online Media
Outsourcing/Offshoring	Package/Freight Delivery
Packaging & Containers	Paper & Forest Products
Performing Arts	Pharmaceuticals
Philanthropy	Photography
Plastics	Political Organization
Primary/Secondary Education	Printing
Professional Trainer and Coach	Program Development
Public Policy	PR and Communications
Public Safety	Publishing
Railroad Manufacture	Ranching
Real Estate	Recreational Facilities & Services
Religious Institutions	Renewables and Environment
Research	Restaurants
Retail	Security and Investigations
Semiconductors	Shipbuilding
Sporting Goods	Sports
Staffing & Recruiting	Supermarkets
Telecommunications	Textiles
Think Tanks	Tobacco
Translation & Localization	Transportation/Trucking/Railroad
Utilities	Venture Capital and Private Equity
Veterinary	Warehousing
Wholesale	Wine and Spirits
Wireless	Writing and Editing

You can't connect the dots looking forward; you can only connect them looking backwards. So you have to trust that the dots will somehow connect in your future.
--Steve Jobs

Select your top five companies, those that align with your career, and, using the search bar, search for people whose profiles have those company names. Read their profiles and connect with them. Build the relationships, research their profiles, and begin to understand your Top Five companies, not from the business side, which you have already done, but from the people side. Get a feel for the people who make up the companies. Let them get to know you! They need you as much as you need them.

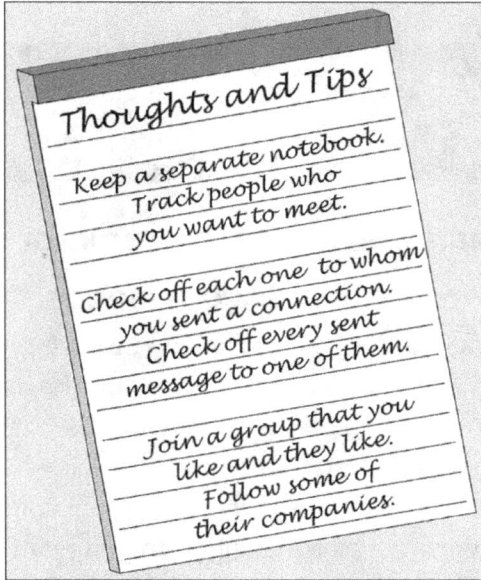

> **Thoughts and Tips**
>
> Keep a separate notebook. Track people who you want to meet.
>
> Check off each one to whom you sent a connection. Check off every sent message to one of them.
>
> Join a group that you like and they like. Follow some of their companies.

Yes, Barbie® has turned 57

That adorable doll that has just turned 55 and has traveled the world with more than 40 nationalities. Barbie® has had more careers than any of us can ever imagine. With over 130 careers she has been a business executive, a doctor, flown to the moon as an astronaut, worked weekends as a cashier at McDonald's, and even been an elementary school teacher. I guess you can say she can teach us a few things about careers. Barbie can also teach us a few things about social media. She plays on Facebook with 13 million fans, 240,000 Twitter followers and over 600,000 followers on Instagram.

Here are This Chapter's Business Consultant Influencers

As you read these profiles, look for possible referrals for your needs.

Is there something in their story you connect with?

Could you gain a new idea or insight for your business or career?

Who do you know or who do they know that can help both of you?

If you needed help or wanted to buy a product, what would it be?

How do you follow up when you meet someone?

When people view your profile, how do you want them to feel?

Do your tribes line up so you could be Power Partners?

What are your favorite questions to ask in an introductory call?

Dr. Benjamin Zvenia

Zvenia and Associates

"A leader is the man who has the ability to get other people to do what they don't want to do and like it." Harry S. Truman

ZVENIA & ASSOCIATES is a law firm guided by Benjamin Zvenia, Dr. P.H., J.D. and the Hon. Norbert Johnson (Ret.). Principals and associates are members of the Federal Circuit Bar Association, FBA, Bar Association of DC, NBA, NNABA, NIBA, OIBA, Bar Association of DC and are admitted in CFR Courts & Tribunals + Tribal Court Systems.

FIRM SPECIALTIES INCLUDE:

U.S. Dept. of Labor Matters including OWCP, EEOICPA. Claims before to NLRB, MSPB, EEOC, OSHA, MSHA, etc. Defense Base Act Claims. Armed Services Board of Contractors Appeals. Our firm also specializes in Native American matters & issues before the Tribal Court Systems including Criminal, Civil, and ICWA. Strengthening Tribal Sovereignty, (for example) Law and Order Code revisions and consultations with Local/State Government. Assisting with Economic Development projects including Tribal and Individual SBA 8a Certification matters. Tribal Workers' Compensation matters (ie., Tribal 1st, etc.). Alternative & Allied Healthcare issues. Social Security Administration claims. Trademark & Copyright Issues. Numerous other federal agency matters (call us for more information). Our firm also provides help with Alternative Dispute Resolution issues.

Dr. Benjamin Zvenia aka
"Helping with all Native American matters & issues that are impacting
today and for generations yet to come."

♟ drzvenia@myfedlawyer.com ♟ 702.384.0991 or 888.809.4305 ♛
www.myfedlawyer.com/ ✓

Robert Adamik

Human Resource Consultant
NeuroLeadership Focus
USC Adjunct Professor

Bob Adamik, aka "Dr. Bob" applied his US Navy leadership skills, as a two-tour Viet Nam Veteran and began his career in a "Fortune 500 and later a Fortune 100 corporation and progressed from Assistant Manager to Senior Vice President of Human Resources. Dr. Bob applied those skills in financial services, banking, credit union and healthcare. He has gained the respect and confidence of virtually thousands of employees in the public and private sector. He has worked in "Start-Up's" and non-profit organizations and continues to be a servant leader while maintaining a Work-Life balance.

He is a Human Resource Generalist building an entire human resource department to include: leadership team development, 360 Degree Feedback, Personality Assessment AVA tools, training and development, talent acquisition, succession planning, and employee relations/legal.

For Life and Career Coaching clients, he uses NeuroLeadership, Neuroscience research, and mindfulness practices to effect change in leaders toward purpose in life and positive outcomes in life.

Robert J. Adamik
linkedin.com/in/drbobadamik
Email robert.adamik1970@gmail.com
Phone: 714-488-1662

The following was found written on the wall in Mother Teresa's home for children in Calcutta:

People are often unreasonable, irrational, and self-centered. Forgive them anyway.

If you are kind, people may accuse you of selfish, ulterior motives. Be kind anyway.

If you are successful, you will win some unfaithful friends and some genuine enemies. Succeed anyway.

If you are honest and sincere people may deceive you. Be honest and sincere anyway.

What you spend years creating, others could destroy overnight. Create anyway.

If you find serenity and happiness, some may be jealous. Be happy anyway.

The good you do today, will often be forgotten. Do good anyway.

Give the best you have, and it will never be enough. Give your best anyway.

In the final analysis, it is between you and God. It was never between you and them anyway.

Mother Theresa

Chapter 10
The Power of Charity and Volunteering

I wouldn't have a veteran live in a home I wouldn't live in myself.
—Larry Thornton

Larry Thornton

CPA for corporations, non-profits, churches CFO, Ridgeview Ranch Treatment Center

My Influencers: Larry Thornton

I love how coincidences work. My friend Shea Vaughn, who is the mom of Vince Vaughn, was going to an army veteran event where I met someone who introduced me to Larry Thornton, who was helping veterans who are homeless or needed recovery.

I decided for myself that I needed to drive all the way to Altadena. That doesn't sound like far but with traffic in LA it could take two hours. I went into this beautiful incredibly professional office and sat down with Larry.

He asked, "Would you like to go see one of our homes?"

Of course, I said, "Yes."

I jumped in this van with three other people and we drove to this beautiful equestrian property in the hills. Across the street I saw a gated multi-million-dollar home. As we walked in, a spiral staircase led to the second floor. To the right was the kitchen. We went upstairs and looked at the beautiful impeccably decorated rooms.

I asked, "Is this where you bring the homeless?"

He said, "I would never have a veteran live in a home I wouldn't live in myself."

Dr. Larry Thornton graduated from the UCLA business administration program and became CEO of multiple companies. He currently has a CPA practice specializing in non-profits, for profit companies and churches. Dr. Thornton has also been a consultant for the Department of Energy, Department of Labor and the Department of Justice in Los Angeles and Washington DC. He was honored as businessman of the year for San Fernando Valley.

Karma is the eternal assertion of human freedom...Our thoughts, our words, and deeds are the threads of the net which we throw around ourselves.
--Swami Vivekananda

He has provided consulting and auditing services for the California Governor, and the Mayor of Los Angeles and currently consults for the Los Angeles City Council regarding veteran housing and drug and alcohol treatment. In addition, he sits on several business and college advisory boards and is CFO of the world-renowned Ridgeview Ranch Treatment Center, a 6-facility drug and alcohol treatment center in Altadena and Pasadena California. He knows a peaceful setting helps with recovery.

Dr. Thornton's love for soldiers started when he was a buffalo soldier himself. He continues to serve the organization as national treasurer overseeing financials for 45 chapters in 38 states.

Attitude of Gratitude

Last year, as I was preparing to send out my annual Thanksgiving letters, I found an old letter in which I wrote about giving thanks to my friends and remembering a time when I had nothing.

One of my girlfriends went to Hawaii for three months and let me live in her condo in Santa Monica. At the time I had no job and no income. The condo was free, but I was still responsible for the electricity, the gas, and the utilities.

Later, as Thanksgiving approached, I called a few of my friends to catch up. I told one of my friends that I wasn't sure what I was going to do about Thanksgiving because my oven didn't work. She told me not to worry, that she had it under control. She brought over a roasting pan (the kind that that you plug in) and a turkey and we roasted the turkey. As I reconnected with my friends in the weeks prior to Thanksgiving, everybody worked together and on the big day, all of them brought food. We created a feast fit for a king! We played games, laughed, and joked. It was the best Thanksgiving ever! It started out as a Thanksgiving where I had nothing and became an incredibly memorable day with friends and food. What more could I have asked for? I was so thankful.

When you approach life with an "attitude of gratitude" you will be surprised at how much you really do have. Changing how you look at life will drive you to be more successful than you ever imagined. Many times, we look at our lives and are unhappy because we're focused on the wrong parts. Focus on the positive, have an attitude of gratitude, and be thankful for what you have.

Tony Robbins, one of my mentors, has a similar mission statement on his Tony Robbins International Basket Brigade website. It is one of the ways Tony Robbins *chooses* to make a difference: "The International Basket Brigade is built on a simple notion: one small act of generosity on the part of one caring person can transform the lives of hundreds." What began as Tony's individual effort to feed families in need has now grown to the point where his campaign provides baskets of food and household items for an estimated two million people annually in countries all over the world.

I'm reminded of my friend, motivational speaker and author Michael J. Herman, who shared a story with me about one Christmas Eve when he and his wife Penny filled up their car with food and from the back of their car fed 68 homeless and hungry people living on Skid Row. Out of that experience of altruism and while creating a project to benefit the community through Landmark Education's Self Expression and Leadership Course, Herman's program, The Needy Smorgasbord Project, was born.

Compassion will cure more sins than condemnation.
--Henry Ward Beecher

The next Christmas Eve, Herman and his wife brought an army of more than 100 friends and volunteers along with donations from almost 50 restaurants and stores to feed homeless, hungry, and needy people. Now this nationwide movement reaches tens of thousands in need. The outcomes were possible because Herman sought to help others. This story of generosity touched me so much that I invited Michael to partner with me on a book about giving and philanthropy.

Can you see how little movements like these can change the world? Can you see how you have within you the greatness and the power to build structures and systems for change and abundance?

Yes, you do!

Helice "Sparky" Bridges   1st
Founder & CEO Difference Makers International
Greater San Diego Area | Nonprofit Organization Management

Current   Difference Makers International

Send a message   Endorse   ▼   **191**
                                                   connections

You Have a Calling

Like random acts of kindness, being at the right place at the right time is critical. My mentor coach Bob Donnell invited me to his inner circle where I met a personality as big as her nickname, Sparky. She gave me a huge heart hug.

"In 1979," she told me, "I was married, had two pre-teen sons, a successful career and a beautiful home overlooking the Pacific Ocean. But no matter how much money I made, I had to live with a husband who controlled, intimidated and verbally abusive me. I was spiritually and emotionally broken. I had no way out. On the very day I decided to commit suicide, I heard a voice inside me say, "You cannot take your life because you are going to make a big difference in the world."

That changed her life. After she divorced her husband, she founded Difference Makers International and created a way to show people how to express appreciation, respect and love for themselves and others which has impacted over 40 million people throughout the world, eradicating bullying, preventing adolescent suicide and helping make dreams come true. She has just launched a global project – One Billion Dreams Coming True by 2020.

Random Acts of Kindness

Since one of my mentors has always been Mother Teresa, I have a huge compassion for the homeless.

I don't if anybody knows the actual percentage of homeless people who are mentally ill. Still, it breaks my heart that they don't know how to properly take care of or fend for themselves. When we care for each other, it's hard for us to see someone else suffering and in need and not take some kind of action.

Since you get more joy out of giving joy to others, you should put a good deal of thought into the happiness that you are able to give.
--Eleanor Roosevelt

One time I was driving by McDonald's and realized my dog needed water, so I ran in quickly to get him some water. Before I could open the door to the restaurant, I saw a homeless woman with different color socks, wearing a poncho, unkempt hair, with a shopping cart filled with her treasures, items others would see as junk.

I instantly stopped and asked her if she was hungry. We caught each other's eyes and she said yes. I thought that buying this woman a meal would be an easy task for me. However, I realized I hadn't gone to the bank and I was standing there with no cash and no debit card.

I decided to use my resourcefulness and ask the cashier if she might have something she could give to this homeless person. She said no. I explained to the cashier that I had no money on me, but this woman was hungry and homeless. She said no again. I asked to see the manager.

The manager came out from behind the counter and in an abrupt manner said, "What do you want?"

I said to him, "There's a homeless woman here who's hungry. You must have something here that can help her. You must have something in the warmer that isn't on order."

He again said no.

"Do you understand that this is a human being who lives in your community? I find it hard to believe you would let someone go hungry."

He said, "It's our policy."

At this point I found myself so frustrated with McDonald's that I started to ask the patrons in the store if they wanted to contribute to buy her lunch. While the woman stood next to me with a sad expression on her face, I asked four tables for help and could not get one person to say yes. I looked at a man who had three cheeseburgers on his tray and asked if he wanted to give her one. He said no.

At this point I was beginning to feel like a failure. All I wanted to do was feed someone who had no food and I couldn't even help this one poor woman. My frantic energy must have been bouncing off the walls. In the distance, I saw an Asian couple and heard them speaking to each other, but I couldn't understand them. For whatever reason, I hadn't bothered to ask them for help knowing it might be difficult for them to understand me.

If you love your freedom thank a Veteran

I have found that among its other benefits, giving liberates the soul of the giver.

--Maya Angelou

However, they did understand my desperate desire. The woman stood and walked over to me and said, "...food...she food...she food?" She pointed at the food and then at the homeless lady.

I said, "Yes, yes," nodding my head up and down.

She said, "I I I," and tapped her chest. All I could say was thank you.

As I watched, the lady told the man, "Meal meal meal," then walked to the counter and bought the homeless lady a meal.

The lady looked at the Asian woman and said, "God bless you."

What's your cause? Helping the homeless, working with underprivileged children, and working with animals that have been rescued are just a few of the causes supported by thousands of charity organizations you can get involved with. Decide what pulls at your heart strings the most and then commit to helping others.

One of my favorite things to do is always carry a protein bar in my glove box. It's simple and easy and it doesn't matter where I am. If I pull into a shopping center and see a homeless person sitting there, I say, "Hey, I have one of these great protein bars. Do you want one?" They almost always say yes.

One day I was eating at a pancake house with my daughter and our breakfast cost $15, which left me with $10. We figured our meal was cheap but her service was extremely top-notch, so we left her the $10 and said, "Thanks! You made our morning delightful." She smiled and said, "You made mine off to a great start."

When we walked out the door we saw a homeless man lying on the grass. He had no socks and his shoes were so worn they looked like they were going to fall off his feet. His hair and beard were both matted and dirty, but through his tattered and torn clothes you could tell they were hanging loose on his body, an indication of malnutrition. It broke my heart, but I had given the waitress the last of my money. I looked around to see if there was another way I could get help for him.

Winners never quit and quitters never win.
--Vince Lombardi

Five different sets of people were standing outside the restaurant waiting for their name to get called to eat their breakfast. I went from family to family asking, "Do you see that homeless man over there? Would you be willing to give him a couple bucks, so he could get something to eat?" One by one they all either said no or turned away, I got so frustrated that people who were going to fill their bellies would allow someone to go hungry right in front of them.

Finally, the door opened and out walked a very young couple. They looked like they were in love or certainly were having a very nice time. I felt silly asking them because it was probably a treat for them to spend the money to go out to breakfast.

I asked anyway. The young man said, "We just used our debit card."

I got it, but then I noticed that they had taken their leftovers. I said, "I know this sounds weird, but do you really think you'll eat those leftovers? I know half the time I think I will eat them but half the time I don't. Why don't you go over there and ask him if he wants them?"

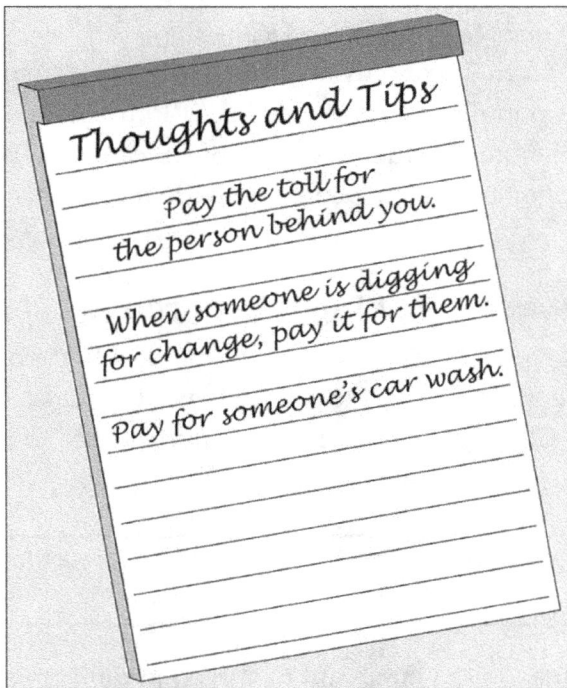

Thoughts and Tips

Pay the toll for the person behind you.

When someone is digging for change, pay it for them.

Pay for someone's car wash.

I had done what I could and walked back to my car. As I got to my car I looked back and saw the homeless guy already eating the food. I smiled ear to ear. I turned the car on, pulled out of the parking lot, and drove down the street. Just as I was about to make a U-turn I heard a honk-honk-honk. It was the young couple, my giving sweet new human connections, waving to me. I could feel their smile and their happiness that they knew they had made a difference.

Later my daughter said, "You know how to bring the best out in people."

I said, "They had greatness in them. "

Even corporations are doing these random acts.

Honda shifted to a Charity message of Random Acts of Helpfulness in its advertising. This brought Honda to the forefront by increasing consumer trust. Local dealer employees went out to the community and washed people's cars, brought nurse, donated needed baby items, and paid for people's parking, while wearing branded light blue polo shirts. They left behind little notes saying, "It's on us." Your Helpful Honda Dealers.

With greater fuel economy and more reliability, small autos have become more popular. JD Power and AARP discovered that people in the 50+ demographic fuel over 60% of US car sales. Honda's new charity message reaches the people who are most likely to buy their cars.

Pay it forward. "Making a Difference"

What has someone done for you in the past that you can do for someone else today? Years ago, I planned to take a trip from California to Chicago, Illinois. I would fly to Chicago and take the train from the airport to my destination.

You can give without loving, but you can never love without giving.
--Robert Louis Stevenson

At that time, I was young and had lived in California most of my life. I was single and was much more concerned to look cute than with the weather. I never even thought about the fact that it was the middle of winter. What did I know about snow? I arrived in Chicago wearing a darling black leather jacket and matching skirt and shoes and transferred from the airport to the train, all without stepping outside. When I arrived at the train station in downtown Chicago I was suddenly outside in 30-degree weather shivering like a chattering monkey.

A lady twice my age said, "Oh my dear, you must be cold."

I was grateful she didn't say, "What in the world are you doing wearing that?" I tried a bit of a laugh and slowly said, "Yeah."

She asked, "Where are you from?"

I said, "Ca-ca-calif-for-ni-a."

She said, "No wonder you are cold." She reached into her bag and said, "Then you must take these."

She pulled out a pair of suede black gloves and handed them to me. To this day I feel like she must have been a guardian angel looking out for me.

Now I know that when the weather gets cold, go to the 99 Cent store where they have two pairs of gloves for $1, grab a bunch and give them to people who look like they need them. Believe me, the smiles they give me are way more valuable than the dollar I spent to help them.

Together we are more

Anytime I go somewhere I keep my ears open and my antennae up. I got an opportunity to go a very large women's conference in Long Beach, produced by Michelle Paterson and formerly produced by Maria Shriver in Long Beach.

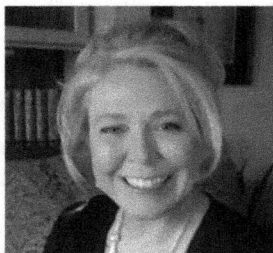

Dee Beaudette

1st

President at Collective Changes, dedicated to supporting global women entrepreneurs through education and mentoring

Greater Seattle Area | Nonprofit Organization Management

Current	Collective Changes, Dee Beaudette Consulting, MacKenzie Romero Consulting
Previous	Peak Education, HIS Foundation, Webster International
Education	Independent Study - AFP Faculty Certification

Send a message   Endorse ▾

500+
connections

Gail M. Romero, CFRE

CEO Collective Changes, NACC Past Board Chair, BM
Gates Foundation - Advisor, Senior Counsel MacKenzie-
Romero Consult

Greater Seattle Area | Executive Office

Current	Bill & Melinda Gates Foundation, Collective Changes - Global Mentoring, Rainmakers tv
Previous	MBA Women International, MBA Women International - formerly NAWMBA, Growing Philanthropy Summit
Education	AFP Faculty Training Academy

Connect | Send Gail InMail ▾

500+
connections

If you're trying to achieve, there will be roadblocks. I've had them; everybody has had them. But obstacles don't have to stop you. If you run into a wall, don't around and give up. Figure out how to climb it, go through it, or work around it.

--Michael Jordan

Among the amazing speakers were Jack Canfield and Lisa Nichols. At one of the booths, I saw a banner that said Collective Changes and curiosity struck. "What was this odd thing about?" I thought. I saw the opportunity, reached out my hand, and said, "Hi, my name is Debra Faris, what's yours?" That's how I met Dee Beaudette.

I was excited as she told me about how Collective Changes became a Global non-profit corporation that empowers women in business through collaboration. "We use a unique on-line and mobile technology to match mentors and mentees. Then we guide them through tasks that build leadership and business skills," she said. "We launched in South Africa and then expanded to help women around the world build and sustain enterprises that create social, political and economic stability."

Dee met Gail in an on-line Master's program at Northpark University in Chicago. Since they both lived on the West Coast, they teamed up to do group projects. After eight years working in different cities, they decided to reconnect and follow their passion for empowering women. Collective Changes was born.

Collective Changes' primary target audience is the forgotten middle women in emerging countries who owning small to medium size enterprises. They complete a six-month program, then continue as associate and then full mentors building leadership skills in their communities.

Social media is an amazing tool, but it's really the face-to-face interaction that makes a long-term impact.
--Felicia Day

Here are This Chapter's Business Consultant Influencers

As you read these profiles, look for possible referrals for your needs.

Is there something in their story you connect with?
Could you gain a new idea or insight for your business or career?
Who do you know or who do they know that can help both of you?
If you needed help or wanted to buy a product, what would it be?
How do you follow up when you meet someone?
When people view your profile, how do you want them to feel?
Do your tribes line up so you could be Power Partners?
What are your favorite questions to ask in an introductory call?

Chris Megison

Helping Solve Homelessness

"It is necessary for us to learn from others' mistakes. You will not live long enough to make them all yourself." Adm Hyman G. Rickover

In 1999, my wife Tammy and I were helping out at an emergency winter shelter with their two boys, when a 9-year old girl named Jessica pulled on my sleeve and innocently asked, "Hey mister, do you live here too?" I looked at the girl and then over to her mother who was preparing a bed on the shelter floor. Getting down on one knee and looking into the girl's eyes, I said, "I don't live here, sweetie, but my wife and I are going to do everything possible so that you, and your family, won't have to live here too."

The girl's eyes welled with tears, and so did mine, and a vision was born—to solve family homelessness. This one night forever changed not only the lives of Jessica and her family, who solved their homelessness, but also the lives of over 2,200 other children and their parents who have since found their way here. Through this promise an imperative evolved that is known today as Solutions for Change.

Today, I'm the President and CEO of Solutions for Change which transforms lives and communities by permanently solving family homelessness. Our approach is unique, providing a complete and sustainable solution driven by accountability.

1.**What discipline could someone learn from you?** Persistence? Courage is being scared to death, but saddling up anyway. (John Wayne)

9.**If you could have any superpower (or be any superhero), what/who would it be and why?** It would be a Magic Civility Wand. Where people could respectfully argue their positions, and hug each other afterwards.

10.**What subject or argument most stirs your emotions, why?** The beast of addiction. It's like a software program with a sneaky code built in; called codependency.

12.**When "winning someone over" do you think facts or emotions carry the day?** Love is an emotion. Love beats any fact, all day, every day.

13.**What do you wish you spent more time doing? What prevents you from doing that now?** Connecting with trailblazers. Too much trailblazing of my own.

14.**In helping others, is it better to teach them, give them, or show them?** It's better to teach the teachers. Or server the servers.

16.**If there were one problem in the world you could solve, what would it be?** Homelessness, but not how most think it should be solved.

Specialties
Helping to permanently solve family homelessness.

Chris Megison aka *"Helping Solve Homelessness"*
Solutions for Change "A Promise to Solve Family Homelessness"
Solving Homelessness Marketing Expert ♚ Self-Development Public Speaking ♕ Personal Spiritual Growth ♔

♜ chris@solutionsforchange.org ♞
www.solutionsforchange.org

Rodney Brown

CEO of New Life Global Development

"Leadership is solving problems the day soldiers have stopped giving you problems is the day you have stopped leading them." Colin Powell

Growing up with my mom and grandmother was violent, bloody and abusive, what seemed like a living hell; while my summers with my grandmother and grandfather on my fathers' side was blissful and heavenly. It was a life of happiness with Christian values and morals this is where I felt the peace of God.

Subsequently, throughout my childhood life I experienced homelessness living on the violent streets of Chicago; however, my close up and personal view of the streets helped me to gain insight of the interconnections between life and humanity. As I matured, I later learned that being exposed to both adversities and blessings of life is what shaped me into a person who is strong minded, compassionate and spiritual, these attributes are the catalysts that has given me the desire and determination to help others.

Today, I'm the CEO of New Life Global Development and a Real Estate Asset Manager, assisting real estate investors in developing affordable housing to support non-profit organizations that serves the homeless.

Specialties: Affordable Housing, Homeless Veterans

Homelessness, Veterans, Homeless Families, Underserved Population, Transitional Aged Youth, Transitional Aged Foster Youth, Ex-Offenders, Senior Citizens, Disabled, VASH Housing, Asset Managers, Real Estate Investors, Property Managers, Affordable Housing Developers, Distress Properties, Trustee Sales, Foreclosures, Bank REO

What books do I recommend? the Holy Bible, Think and Grow Rich, Dreams into Actions (Getting what you want)
With what "LinkedIn Influencer" do you resonate and what character trait do you share? Michael Josephson, he is an ethicist-CEO and founder of Joseph Institute of Ethics. Traits we share are ethics and good character.
If you could be anyone for a day, who would it be and what experience can you envision? Dr. Ben Carson, The US Secretary of Housing, I would envision for that day influence all of powers to change laws and policies on affordable housing.
If you could have any superpower (or be any superhero), what/who would it be and why? The superpower would be mind control, to assist those who don't understand to do the right thing
What subject or argument most stirs your emotions, why? The mistreatment of children seniors' citizens, because of the absence of voice.
In helping others, is it better to teach them, give them, or show them? Teach them, because teaching them helps them to develop a life skill.
If there were one problem in the world you could solve, what would it be? Hatred

Rodney Brown
"Housing is a Human Right"
♛ Real Estate Asset Management ♟ Project Manager ♛ Real Estate Development ♟ Solving Homeless Housing Programs
♟ rcipartnersllc@gmail.com ♟ 310-351-4631

Chapter 11
Entrepreneurship & Mentors

I knew that if I failed I wouldn't regret that, but I knew the one
thing I might regret is not trying.
--Jeff Bezos, founder and CEO Amazon.com

Jeff Hoffman

**Entrepreneur (Priceline, Ubid, etc.)
Worldwide Motivational Speaker
Film, TV & Music Producer**

My Influencers: Jeff Hoffman

With half a billion people on LinkedIn you never know who you're going to find on the biggest professional social business platform in the world. Back in 2014 I connected with Jeff Hoffman on LinkedIn after going to an event which was called the Big Money Speaker. When Jeff spoke, I knew he was a global speaker, did TedTalks and spoke at Ivy League schools like Harvard & Stanford which was huge because I wanted to be a speaker.

I realized he was the biggest Entrepreneur I ever met. How many people have you met that were not just talking about their Million-dollar ideas but actually implemented Billion-dollar companies?

Called one of the most influential Tech Guys in America Jeff Hoffman is a successful entrepreneur, proven CEO, worldwide motivational speaker, published author, In his career, he has been the founder of multiple startups, he has been the CEO of both public and private companies, and he has served as a senior executive in many capacities. Jeff has been part of a number of well-known successful startups, including Priceline.com/Booking.com, uBid.com and more.

Jeff serves on the boards of companies in the US, Europe, the Middle East, South America, Africa, and Asia. He supports entrepreneurs and small businesses on a worldwide basis. He is the Chief Evangelist and a founding board member of the Global Entrepreneurship Network, which works with entrepreneurs in 175 countries, as well as being a founding board member of The Unreasonable Group. He supports the White House, the State Department, the United Nations, and similar organizations internationally on economic growth initiatives and entrepreneurship programs.

Jeff was honored with the Champion of Entrepreneurship Award from JP Morgan Chase and Citibank, as well as receiving a Lifetime Achievement Award and being inducted into the Entrepreneurs Hall of Fame.

Outside of the world of technology, he produced a Grammy winning jazz album, an Emmy Award winning television show and movies in Hollywood, He has also produced musical events including concerts, tours, and charity events with such artists as Elton John, Britney Spears, NSYNC, Boyz II Men, and others, and serves on numerous charity and non-profit boards.

I am telling you to make a choice based on your passions and interests, not what everyone else is telling you to do. It doesn't work that way. You wind up living a life for the wrong reasons, and you never get the most out of it. Just always think about why you are doing what you are doing.

--Jeff Hoffman

Questions are the Answer

When I go to an event, I always ask myself what the most important thing I learned was. At a Tony Robbins seminar 20 years ago, I learned a set of questions and a mindset that I still use today:

What is your purpose, what is your intention, and questions are the answers.

Here's how you do it differently. You ask yourself, "What's my purpose and what's my intention?" Your answer might be, "My purpose is to meet people I can build relationships with that further my purpose to find a job for a client."

Discipline is the bridge between goals and accomplishment.
--Jim Rohn

Is that part of your intention? No. Your intention might be, "I'm going to look for ways in which I can better serve my clients, so I've compiled a list of 20 things I did in the past that didn't help my clients."

Coming together is a beginning; keeping together is a progress; Working together is success.
--Henry Ford

When you do this, ask, "What are the questions that I can ask a person attending this event?" That would be far more productive. One of Stephen Covey's most important mindsets is, "First seek to understand then to be understood." If you invest in the people you want to meet and help and not in your own story, you will be far more successful.

Recently, I transformed a client's job-seeking world from networking for two years with no success to getting a job within 60 days. Here is how I did it. I asked an audience, "How many of you go to networking events?" I knew the answer. They all raised their hands and said they network. The error they make is that networking is not the end; it's a means to the end. It gives you the opportunity to meet people and build relationships. True networking results from qualifying and building the relationships you start at the networking event.

Questions are the answer to your problems. They are everything. No matter where you go, it is all about the questions. If your intention is finding members of your market, start asking questions that will draw the people you are trying to attract to you.

When Tony Robbins taught me about questions and answers, he instilled in me the idea that we need to ask the right questions of ourselves and of others to get the best possible answers. When you do this right, you will forge the strongest possible relationships with others and with yourself.

The best investment you can make in yourself is getting to know yourself. Read books, take risks, and get involved in clubs that will teach you leadership. There you will discover the skills you do and do not possess and which skills you must acquire.

Jack Canfield says, "Everything you want in life is just outside your comfort zone." Step outside your normal circle of friends, your normal habits, and your normal cycle. Stretch yourself and then ask yourself how the experience felt. Analyze it by asking yourself if it made you feel inferior in some areas and superior in others. By doing this you learn and grow. You can then bring these lessons to the table when you go on interviews or sales calls.

What is ROI vs. ROT

In the finance and investment world, everyone thinks return on your investment (ROI). In the networking world, people will network and network and have nothing to show for the time invested. They neglect that most important metric, Return on Your Time (ROT).

Here is the full story of how I transformed a friend's job seeking world from networking for two years with no results to getting a job within 60 days.

Since I know a lot of people who don't take their networking to a deep enough level or qualify the time spent against the results achieved, I quickly recognized his problem.

I asked my friend, "How many networking events do you go to a week?"

He answered, "Five to seven."

I asked him, "What does your wife say when you get home?"

He answered, "She asks me how it went."

I asked, "And your reply?"

"Okay."

"*Wow!*" I said. "Let's do the math. Say you attend three events a week and it takes you an hour and half to get ready and to drive there. Is that fair?"

He said, "Yes."

I said, "You probably spend at least an hour and a half, right? That's about 12 hours a week looking for a job, and you only worked with three events."

This shows that with an effective profile on LinkedIn and connections in place, you can reach hundreds of companies in a short period of time. With recommendations from former colleagues and bosses, influencers who share your vision, and endorsements for your skills, potential employers will get a feel for who you are, to what you're committed and whether you're a good fit for their organization or not. In the current job market, as in every past era, the best way to get a job is to find a connection with more celebrity in your field than you have who can promote you inside a company or who has connections inside the company.

Internet searches and posting resumes to hundreds of companies is a thing of the past. Using your connections and resources is the way to get your next job. Through the networking and profiling available on LinkedIn, you will be ahead of the others.

Strategize your Success

When McDonald's spends a million dollars to build a new store, they position it carefully, on a corner if possible, near an intersection if they can, so it is easily visible to oncoming traffic. If you sit at a traffic light for one or two minutes, your brain may notice a McDonald's down the road and say, "McDonald's! I'm hungry!"

Many times, people find themselves in the parking lot of a McDonald's or other fast food place they had no intention of visiting. Very few of them leave the house saying, "I'm going to McDonald's today," but they wind up there anyway.

Some people know that if they plan to eat a healthy lunch, they need to pack their lunch; which means planning ahead and buying healthy foods. When people make this commitment, they know what their bodies need and make health a high-level value.

Both examples represent a strategic plan. McDonald's uses strategy to place its restaurants in the right spot to get people to stop. The person who packs their lunch uses a different strategy. To succeed in life, you too must adopt a strategy.

The same thing happens on LinkedIn. To be successful using LinkedIn you must adopt a strategy. Yours may differ from your roommate's. Start with the end in mind, work backwards and let LinkedIn work for you. Use the strategies I have outlined in this book to build a plan to connect with the best people in your industry, develop local and the national celebrity connections, use those connections to get in the door, then let your knowledge and ideas sine in the interview that will land you your ideal job.

Billion Dollar Mindset

One of my favorite people from *The Secret* is John D. Martini. John mentioned that *The Secret* told a lot of great stories about universal laws, but he adds the action steps needed to get to the end in mind. This process is how billionaires make their billions of dollars.

One billionaire he talks about is Warren Buffet. People wonder how successful people become successful. At age 11 Warren Buffet read every book on finance in the Nebraska State Library in Omaha. No wonder Warren Buffet is worth $50 billion dollars. This Billionaire Circle and includes members such as Buffet, Richard Branson, Donald Trump, Sara Blakely, (the youngest female billionaire), Bill Gates, and Steve Jobs. Even if you don't have the desire to become a billionaire, the success principles they use will lead you to success.

Before 1954, nobody had run a mile in under four minutes. Many people, including doctors, believed it was impossible for a human being to run that fast. Roger Bannister ignored all the naysayers and in 1954 broke the four-minute barrier. Since then, over 20,000 people have reached that seemingly unreachable goal.

Les Brown says that everything is possible. Everything you need is already inside you, waiting to be used. When you operate out of your imagination and not your memory, you will see possibilities everywhere and will be able to act on them.

Think about what people are doing on Facebook today. They're keeping up with their friends and family, but they're also building an image and identity for themselves, which in a sense is their brand. They're connecting with the audience that they want to connect to.
--Mark Zuckerberg

Why it is important to me to show you that my awareness to the billionaire circle is twofold?

1. I didn't know that there are over 1,645 billionaires. Did you? Awareness is the first step to learning everything including yourself.

2. When you played the "I am" game (your character traits), you helped yourself get clear of who you are, so you can authentically share with other in order for them to get to know you better. With millionaires and billionaires their characteristics and skills will help you to see, if you see greatness in others you can see it in yourself. What other possibilities could this create for you?

Here are a few billionaires

Giorgio Armani- Fashion Designer

Jeff Bezos- Amazon

Liliane Bittencourt- L'Oreal

Sara Blakley- Spanx (youngest female billionaire)

Michael Bloomberg- Bloomberg LP (stock market)

Donald Bren- Real Estate
Sergey Brin- Google
Warren Buffet- Berkshire Hathaway
Michael Dell- Dell computers
Larry Ellison-Oracle
Bill Gates- Microsoft
Reid Hoffman- LinkedIn
Steve Jobs- Apple
Phil Knight- Niki
Eric Lefkosky- Groupon
Forrest Mars- Candy
Dietrich Mateschitz- Red Bull
Howard Schultz- Starbucks
Donald Trump- Television, Real Estate
Christy Walton- Walmart
Ty Warner- Beanie Babies
Mark Zuckerberg- Facebook

Who's Your Wingman?

One of my favorite movies from the 80's, *Top Gun*, depicts this next concept very nicely. The movie pairs Maverick, an egotistical fighter pilot, with Goose, his co-pilot/navigator. The two are inseparable. They compete with another pair of aviators at the top of their game as well, led by Iceman. Maverick and Iceman are rivals who don't care for each other. They have extremely different styles, different agendas, and clash at every opportunity. By the end of the movie, the two have resolved their differences and come to acknowledge that each has valuable skills. One of the best lines comes from Maverick after they've engaged in a dogfight with enemy aircraft. He looks at Ice and says, "You can be my wingman any time." Ice responds with, "No, you can be mine!" It shows that the two have figured out how to work together and to succeed.

Your wingman is a person you can count on, who is willing to take great risks for you, and who will ensure that you reach your goal. Who is your wingman? Like Maverick and Ice, you may start out rocky, but develop a bond that is strong and able to withstand anything. Develop strong, lasting relationships through LinkedIn and you will find that your wingmen will help you get the job you seek.

Social Trailblazers

Social media is social business. There's a misconception that LinkedIn isn't social media and can be used only as a business network. However, like Facebook, LinkedIn is used to connect with others, including other veterans, and start conversations and is an acceptable form of social media.

Good leadership consists of showing average people how to do the work of superior people.
--John D. Rockefeller

People have been in the business of being social since business began. From playing golf with doctors to weekend cocktail parties at the office, the social aspect is a huge part of business. With the addition of the Internet, social interactions have stepped onto a whole new platform and expanded to include multi-media sites that make it easier than ever to reach people globally. Each platform has its strengths in different industries and genres. Some of my friends on different platforms are highly successful business people.

John Chow 1st
Founder & CEO at TTZ Media, Inc.
Vancouver, Canada Area | Internet

Current   TTZ Media Inc., John Chow dot Com, TTZ Media, Inc.

Send a message   Endorse ▾   500+
                                      connections

We all know how popular blogging has become. From Fortune 500 companies to our favorite health television show, Dr. Oz, everyone is blogging or reading blogs, most of them on WordPress.

My favorite blogger is my friend John Chow, who I have lunch with on a regular basis and whose daughter plays with my dog from time to time. John talks about everyday stuff on his blog. Several times, I've seen him post photos of his lunch on his blog.

Smart phones and social media expand our universe. We can connect with others or collect information easier and faster than ever.
--Daniel Goleman

Mia Voss
1st

The Mia Connect & Host of "TMC OnAir"
Google+/YouTube Programs. @TheMiaConnect
Greater Denver Area | Management Consulting

Current	The Mia Connect, TMC Services LLC, CRAVE Denver
Previous	The Neenan Company, OZ Architecture - Denver, Gryphon Development

Send a message   Endorse ▾

500+
connections

Mari Smith
1st

Facebook Marketing Expert Author & Trainer | Social Media Speaker | Relationship Marketing Specialist
Greater San Diego Area | Internet

Current	Mari Smith	Social Media Speaker & Consultant	Facebook Marketing Expert
Previous	Social Media Examiner, Facebook Marketing: An Hour A Day
Education	Elementary = BC, Canada; High School = Edinburgh, Scotland

Send a message ▾

500+
connections

My favorite Facebook person is Mari Smith, who wrote *Facebook for Dummies*.

As we move further into the twenty-first century, the internet will continue to become more and more a way to communicate, network, and build relationships. Although each site is designed with a specific purpose, in general they all work to connect people and share communications with others.

Joel Comm
1st

New York Times Best-Selling Author | International Keynote Speaker | Entrepreneur | New Media Marketing Strategist

Greater Denver Area | Information Technology and Services

Current	Joel Comm, Inc., a Joel Comm Company	International Conference & Keynote Speaker	Corporate Events, InfoMediaInc.com, a Joel Comm Company; Joel Comm is an International Public Keynote Speaker
Previous	Digital Future, Inc., a Joel Comm Company; Joel is an international motivational speaker, ClassicGames.com	Acquired by Yahoo as Yahoo! Games (Joel is now a keynote & motivational speaker)
Education	University of Illinois at Urbana-Champaign

Send a message ▼

500+

In the Twitter world, blogging is content driven with short and sweet tweets, tiny snippets ending with a hash tag or a link. Twitter is very popular in the job world. Joel Com uses Twitter very effectively for his business. In the Google Plus world they love their Google hangouts and You Tube.

Jack C Crawford
1st

Senior Director at Cognizant Technology Solutions ∴ Advisory Consultant, Customer Solutions Practice

Greater Los Angeles Area | Information Technology and Services

Current	Cognizant Technology Solutions
Previous	Allergan, 2-1-1 Orange County, OC Partnership to End Homelessness
Education	Claremont Graduate University

Send a message ▼

500+
connections

My dear friend Jack Crawford uses Google Plus regularly and speaks to and interviews many people through Google Hangouts.

Mia Voss uses Google Hangouts for interviews and meetings. You can use your media link from You Tube to post interviews for Google Hangout on your LinkedIn profile.

Here are This Chapter's Business Consultant Influencers

As you read these profiles, look for possible referrals for your needs.

Is there something in their story you connect with?
Could you gain a new idea or insight for your business or career?
Who do you know or who do they know that can help both of you?
If you needed help or wanted to buy a product, what would it be?
How do you follow up when you meet someone?
When people view your profile, how do you want them to feel?
Do your tribes line up so you could be Power Partners?
What are your favorite questions to ask in an introductory call?

Gregory Taylor
President at
TTT Veterans Wellness LCC

Experienced President with a demonstrated history of working in the alternative medicine industry / Telecommunications. President and Co-Founder of the Black Student Union, Whittier College. Strong Advocate for Homeless Veterans and Veterans Alike. Skilled in Customer Service, Strategic Planning, Software Project Management, Team Building, Public Speaking, International Speaking, and Peer Support. A business development professional with a Bachelor of Science in Social Psychology and Political Science. A Strong Advocate for Human Rights and public awareness in Strategic Community Redevelopment. i.e.: Homeless Veterans Rights and Affairs. Commissioner for the 64th District, City of Los Angeles.

TTT Veterans Wellness helps to empower Veterans to recover and effectively reintegrate them back into their communities.

We believe Veterans and their families deserve a coordinated effort to find secure housing, mental health counseling, employment and empowerment.

We respond to Veterans issues of reconnecting to family life. TTT Veterans Wellness Program recognizes that addressing the need for information and accessing resources are important parts of helping.

Gregory Taylor
linkedin.com/in/gregory-taylor-6a78b7153

Man is not born
to solve the problems
of the universe,
but to find out
what he has to do...
within the limits
of his comprehension.

Johann Wolfgang
von Goethe

Chapter 12
Reinventing Yourself & Beyond

Courage is not the absence of fear, but rather the judgment that something else is more important than fear..

--Janet Chin

Janet Chin

**Civilian Aide to the
Secretary of the Army (California)**

My Influencers: Janet Chin

As the daisy chain goes, my friend Jesse Medina invited me to a military event where Janet Chin was speaking. I found long ago that speakers and authors are experts in their craft and know other great connections. I waited to meet Janet to find not only her brilliance assisting veterans but also her alliance with dignitaries. We later went together to watch John Shin (known for *Think and Grow Rich* . In England he was Knighted along with his wife being Damed.

After the meeting, I asked her, "Why did you join the service?"

"I was the youngest daughter of my Dad's seven children and the only one that chose to serve in the military.

"I remembered him religiously watching M.A.S.H. episodes on TV. He also had a scar on his arm from where he was grazed by a bullet saving the life of his battle buddy. When asked about it, he would tell me that serving in the Army was the best time in his life.

As a young child, I was a justice seeker, protecting the "shy" kids in my class and standing up to anyone who disrespected my mother who was a domestic violence survivor. When my dad passed away, we lived off welfare, Social Security benefits, and my mom even dumpster dived from time to time to make ends meet.

Many people may be embarrassed to let others know, but I find those aspects of my life helped me be more compassionate and connected to those less fortunate. I also acknowledged how I was embarrassed to watch my mom and occasionally help her get vegetables and bruised fruit out of the dumpsters. I felt ashamed and "less" than my peers. I was determined to change my trajectory and pivot when things in my life felt wrong.

At age 17, I enlisted in the Army. I picked S. Korea as my first duty station.

I joined the service to stand out from my high school peers. The Army adventure and challenge was so appealing, that I enlisted when I turned age 17. My mom had to sign my enlisted documents, since I was still underaged. I knew that when I made up mind that I was never going to regret passing on the opportunity to serve in uniform. I knew uniformed services was special and I was drawn to the challenge to achieve something bigger and greater than the world I knew.

"My affirmation in life has been a journey of service and I am grateful every day to be able to contribute something. The calling to serve and to be of service to another person was my most important take away from serve in the Army."

"What did you do in the service and how did it create part of your Character Traits?"

"I enlisted as a E-2 (Private) to the Signal Corps and was trained as a 74C (Record Telecommunications Center Operator) I primarily worked in a communications center both in a "bunker" and in "tactical" settings. I drove a 5 Ton truck with a communications shelter on it as part of a rapid response unit. My team and I routed top secret messages all around the world and was basically the internet before the internet came into the public realm.

The Army is an amazing organization and I am blessed to have experienced its operations from the inside, outside, from afar, and through the eyes of the public. The Army is about people.

The work ethic of showing up on time, completing the mission, and repeating taught me responsibility and the importance of being dependable which I have encompassed into three words that I practice daily: Character, Respect, Gratitude.

The breakdown is simple:

1.   Character of a self that includes a natural curiosity to learn, explore, discover, and share.

2.   Respect for self and others that includes perspectives different than your own and a need for commonality.

3.   Gratitude for all things and to simply voluntarily give back, connect with, and pay it forward.

Coaches, Mentors & Role Models

When we develop habits, those habits control our destiny. This is why people who make millions of dollars are willing to pay a coach one thousand dollars a month without thinking anything of it to keep themselves on track, taking the actions they commit to taking.

Building these habits is a lifetime endeavor. That's why one of the best things you can do is hire a coach to keep on track as you build the record that will make you a prime candidate for new jobs. You need this coaching support because it is so easy to get sidetracked when you're not supported by a structure that tells you what to do every day.

One of my favorite people to go to lunch with during events is Kory Minor. I met Kory a few years back and had no idea who he was. At a recent speaking event, we bumped into each other and talked for a few minutes. I realized he was charming, funny, and down to earth.

I asked him, "What did you do in your previous life?"

He responded, "I was a linebacker and special teams player for the San Francisco 49ers."

I was so excited because I'm from the Bay area. As we talked, I asked Kory what he was most proud of in his life. He said that he was a blessed man because he received a full scholarship to Notre Dame University. He played football for the Irish and got an amazing education. We then moved on to Kory's mentor, Les Brown, who coincidentally is one of my mentors and one of my favorite people.

The price of success is hard work, dedication to the job at hand, and the determination that whether we win or lose, we have applied the best of ourselves to the task at hand.
--Vince Lombardi

I asked him, "How and why did you make the transition from football to speaker?"

He thought for a moment and then said, "Everybody gets knocked down and we all have to get back up. Not everybody has an easy childhood and some of us come from the wrong side of the tracks. But everyone fights adversity."

Kory explained that his biggest fear is the fear of failure. He had a strong desire to create his own legacy and a dream of becoming an entrepreneur. Kory is the Founder and CEO of Kory Minor Industries (www.koryminor.com) which is a personal development and training company working with individuals and organizations to "get off the sideline and get into the game." He has written the book *Make a Touchdown of Your Life* and believes that you have greatness inside you. Kory says there are four pieces to the success puzzle:

1. Have a game plan
2. Take action
3. Fight through adversity
4. Be adaptable

Kory sees life as a vessel to help others. He believes that if you have the right play and follow the right steps you can make a touchdown of your life. Kory's big goal is to teach teenagers financial literacy. He believes that smart people use their brains make a difference.

Les Brown is one of my favorite mentors. He has worked with many generations and inspired many people. When you watch Les Brown speak you can feel the energy he generates. He is filled with passion and gives deep, emotional speeches. At one point, I had the opportunity to have dinner with him. A friend invited me to meet up with her and it turns out that her husband was getting private coaching from Les Brown. They invited me to dinner and it was such an honor to have dinner with one of my greatest role models. There were just 10 of us there and it is an experience I will never forget.

How the Internet Changed Opportunities

In today's world, information is at your fingertips. Want to find a place to eat? Search for one and within a minute you will have more choices than you know what to do with.

The internet has also changed the way we learn. We have developed technologies and systems that extend education to a larger group of people. Online classes for people of all ages are becoming more and more popular. Changes are coming so fast with the internet that not only is education available, education companies are finding ways to increase and improve the outcomes that internet education can deliver.

> *When you believe you can – you can!*
> **--Maxwell Maltz**

In 2004 Salman Kahn began posting math tutorial videos on You Tube. From these videos, he developed the Kahn Academy, a carefully structured series of educational videos offering complete curricula originally in math but now in additional subjects as well. He teaches through the videos and shows the power of interactive exercises. He's flipping the current education model and asks teachers to create video lectures the students can watch at home while doing homework in class where they can ask questions and get help.

> *Leadership is the art of getting someone else to do something you want done because he wants to do it.*
> **--Dwight D. Eisenhower**

The teachers that use Kahn's videos are using technology to humanize the classroom. The one-size-fits-all lectures are gone, replaced by students interacting with one another to learn. One of Kahn's biggest supporters in this new form of education is Bill Gates. The Kahn Academy is a non-profit organization with significant funding from the Bill & Melinda Gates Foundation, Ann and John Doer, Lemann Foundation, and Google.

In addition to new ways of learning, students have access to more information than ever before. Projects and reports that used to be taxing have become much simpler due to the internet. Articles and books are online and easily accessible. Knowledge is at everyone's fingertips. You step out and search for it.

Visions & Visualizations

In the movie *The Secret*, there's a scene where John Assaraf had just moved into his new home and was unpacking boxes in his office. His son walked in to help him unpack. He pulled a large board with pictures and words pasted on it out of a box. "Wow, my old vision board," he said. "It's been years since I looked at this."

"What's a vision board, Dad?" his son asked.

John Assaraf   1st [in]

CEO, PraxisNow | Built 5 Multi-Million Dollar Companies | Philanthropist | NY Times Best Selling Author

Rancho Santa Fe, California | Professional Training & Coaching

Current	PraxisNow
Previous	RIA Ventures, Inc., IPIX Corporation, RE/MAX of Indiana
Education	Montreal Canada

Send a message   Endorse   ▾   **500+**
                                                   connections

"A vision board is a place where you put your dreams," he said. "You write down or add photos of the stuff you want to accomplish, and it helps you work toward it."

Failure is the opportunity to more intelligently begin again.
-Henry Ford

He opened the box and pulled out the vision board that he had created five years earlier. As he turned the board around his son gasped. There on the board was a photo of the house they had just moved into. Five years earlier, John had put his house on the vision board, and his vision had just come true. What a coincidence.

Recently I stayed at my friend Stephanie's house in Laguna Niguel, California, just south of Los Angeles, for the weekend. When I arrived, she met me at the door and said, "I got you a spot under the stars."

"What do you mean?" I replied.

"I got you a spot under the stars. Follow me." We headed down the hall to an amazing room with huge windows and a soft fluffy bed piled with pillows. I thought, "This is amazing." Then I looked up and saw stars above my head. I thought I was in heaven!

After a night of wonderful dreams in an amazing room under the stars, I woke up refreshed. I looked around and on her bookshelf, saw

John Assaraf's book, *The Vision Board Book*. What a coincidence. John Assaraf and I had connected through LinkedIn.

My friend Stephanie arrived and saw me with the book. "I see you got into my books," she said.

"I'm a book nut. I love this book and John Assaraf is one of my connections on LinkedIn." I then shared the story of the vision board and the house with Stephanie.

"I'm in that book," she said.

"No way!" I said.

"I'm in that book," she said again.

Again, I said, "No way!"

"I'm in that book. There's a story about how I trained to compete in the Ironman Competition."

It finally sunk in. My friend Stephanie was in this book! She told me the whole story. She had done several triathlons and had just finished a race in Boston. Shortly after that race, she received a call informing her that she had qualified for the Ironman Competition in Hawaii. This worldwide competition has only 1,500 spots available. She had just qualified for one of those spots. They needed one question answered immediately, "Are you in or will you pass?"

If you can get better at your job, you should be an active member of LinkedIn, because LinkedIn should be connecting you to the information, insights, and people to be more effective.
-Reid Hoffman

An answer right now, she thought, okay, when opportunity knocks just say yes. She said yes. She had just committed to this event, but then realized she had no idea what she had committed to. What was an Ironman? Where was it? When was it? She had no clue that she had just committed herself to an Ironman competition in Hawaii in 45 days.

Once she figured out that it was a triathlon that included three events, a 2.4-mile swim, a 112-mile bike race, and a 26.2-mile marathon, she realized she had to do something drastic.

She had never done anything remotely like this. Most athletes train for the Ironman for a year or two. She had 45 days. She went to the one person she knew who could help her, a friend who trained athletes on visualization. This friend agreed to help her train for her Ironman and they began with very specific drills and training for both the mind and body. She had to condition her mind to see the result before she could get her body in shape in 45 days. She focused on seeing herself in the race, seeing her body in condition for the race, and felt herself running the race.

The power of our mind, the biggest muscle we possess, is incredible. She performed a successful Ironman because she stayed focused and trained her mind to get her to where she needed to be physically.

Looking Outside the Box

Thinking outside the box is a key to success. When you are creative as you work on your career, you will find solutions and answers others won't bother to seek out for themselves.

Earlier in this book I showed you that questions are the answer. If you understand this aphorism, it will change your world. It's not what you know that's important; it's what you don't know that you need to know that will be critical to your success. Ask yourself questions about where you want to work and what type of work you want to do. Then dig for solutions. Use LinkedIn to help in your quest. You will have millions of people, industries, jobs, and employers at your fingertips. Use your ingenuity and the relationships that you've built find new solutions to old problems. If I reach out to the CEO, will he answer me? These are a few examples of questions you can ask yourself to begin thinking outside the box and setting up your life in the manner you desire.

When you search for your next job, LinkedIn gives you a detailed roadmap that will guide you through the maze of companies where you could play your desired role.

Think Tank & Mastermind

Imagine that you just took a trip around the world with eight of the smartest people in the world. Would you see things from a different perspective?

I met Roger Salam at a Tony Robbins event 30 years ago and knew without a shadow of doubt that he was a difference maker.

As years passed I decided to make a list of people I had met back then since I wondered where they were.

One by one found them. When Roger reappeared, I was not surprised that he had become an international speaker and author, worked directly with Tony Robbins, and did 3,700 talks. As founder of The Winner Circle runs the most unique mastermind event in the world at a 38,000 square-foot mansion.

One of the challenges in networking is everybody thinks it's making cold calls to strangers. Actually, it's the people who already have strong trust relationships with you, who know you're dedicated, smart, and a team player, who can help you.
-- Reid Hoffman

Recently, I was part of an all the star lineup and got to speak at icon event with my long-lost friend Roger "Wajed" Salam. Roger says that positioning is key when forming a mastermind group. You look at the result you want to achieve to create your vision and mission. Individual goals may very but your core values and principles must align.

Roger says a core 100 people who are aligned can mastermind together and influence millions. My favorite quotes are, "Who you hang with, who you associate with, and who you listen to will determine your destiny" and "None of us is as smart as all of us."

Amazing Grace, a Pondering Thought

Amazing Grace by John Newton is an amazing song sung in hundreds of churches all over the world. Yet most people are not aware of the deep sorrow attached to it, the many lives that were lost, and the stories behind them. The even more astounding but extremely thought-provoking paradox is how we... you... me... each one of us... can change or be difference makers.

In the mid eighteenth century, John Newton, age 22, was a slave trader exporting human lives from West Africa to South Carolina on his own slave ship. One night he had a dramatic faith experience during a storm at sea. Following that storm, he gave his life to God and began to read spiritual books and pray. He continued to run his slave ships, making three more voyages. Two days before his fourth voyage was to set sail, a mysterious illness temporarily paralyzed him. He never made the fourth journey.

That experience changed his life, which changed his thinking. He became a pastor who opposed the slave trade. In 1788 he met William Wilberforce, an influential Member of Parliament, and began to mentor him on the slave trade. The two men collaborated in a campaign to outlaw the slave trade. In 1807 the once sinner Newton along with Wilberforce and their colleagues prevailed when Parliament voted to outlaw the slave trade in Britain. He almost single-handedly abolished slavery. The sinner became one of the most influential humanitarians of his time and the ripple effect of his actions changed the world.

Most of us fail to question how it happens that people can create such devastating life events as slavery and how we can prevent such moral failings in the future. John Newton was born into the slave trade. At the age of 11 in 1743, he went to sea with his father to Jamaica as a slave master. He became a midshipman, was demoted for trying to desert, and then returned to West Africa on another slave ship.

Many people go through tragedies and hardships that other people who haven't walked in their shoes cannot understand. These others are filled with judgment and criticism because they take their everyday freedom for granted and do not realize what it took for the person they criticize to get where they are.

We all have been involved in judgment and criticism and even condemnation toward another person because we believe they should or should not have done something.

Dr. Wayne Dyer shared in his program *Wishes Fulfilled* that as soon as he let go his self-defeating inflections, he created miracles in his life. We are all just doing what we know how to do. (paraphrased) "We must let go of any thoughts of judgment, criticism or condemnation. We are all God's children," he says.

Here are This Chapter's Business Consultant Influencers

As you read these profiles, look for possible referrals for your needs.

Is there something in their story you connect with?

Could you gain a new idea or insight for your business or career?

Who do you know or who do they know that can help both of you?

If you needed help or wanted to buy a product, what would it be?

How do you follow up when you meet someone?

When people view your profile, how do you want them to feel?

Do your tribes line up so you could be Power Partners?

What are your favorite questions to ask in an introductory call?

3

Robert Stohr

**Director U.S.VETS Patriotic Hall Site
at U.S.VETS Initiative**

"Leadership is solving problems the day soldiers have stopped giving you problems is the day you have stopped leading them." Colin Powell

Strategic creative leader for non-profit work with excellent clinical psychological skills. I'm also an active Marriage, Family, and Child Therapist with an interest and specialization in relationship counseling, LGBTQ issues, working with Suicide Loss Survivors, and Suicide Attempt Survivors.

Specialties: Providing leadership to U.S. VETS in external programs including U.S. VETS Veterans Service Center at Patriotic Hall, Supportive Services for Veterans Families, Outside the Wire and Regional Workforce Initiatives.

Evaluating community needs and help develop programs to meet those needs. Establishing partnerships with community and local agencies and developing a database of services within the homeless continuum of care.

Establishing relationships with state, and local coalitions. Developing a database of legislative contacts interested in issues of homelessness and veterans. Ensuring core values maintained within all partnership activities.

Grant writing as it relates to community partnerships. Assisting in preparing annual budgets for related projects. Ensuring organizational policy compliance in all collaborations. Regularly assessing all partnerships for benefit to the organization and to homeless and at-risk veterans and progress towards objectives with effective outcomes. Providing necessary management and technical assistance to staff. Managing regular communication with community partners. Acting as spokesperson for the organization as required. Providing services to homeless and at-risk veterans in the community by participating in outreach, service events, and problem solving.

Robert Stohr
♕ Veteran Leadership ♔ Meeting Community Needs ♕ Establishing Partnerships ♔ Grant Writing
65♖ ♞

Chapter 13
Veteran Advocates

Chris Naugle

**CEO, Flipout Academy
Real Estate Investment Strategist**

My Influencers: Chris Naugle

On my way to an event with my friend Riadh Handi, he's an Instagram fanatic, he asked me if we could bring his friend who was in town from New York. As we talked in the car I found that his friend Chris Naugle had a television show. He kept saying his goal was to really help people that don't have a lot of money to flip houses. Then he said, "I'd love to help Veterans and make a difference."

He was raised in a lower middle-class family where no one in his extended family was wealthy or even came close. At only 16 years old Chris promised himself he would never work for anyone else ever again. With a $500 loan from the bank and backed by a dream, Chris started a small clothing line in his mother's basement that soon turned into a WNY chain of skateboard and snowboard stores.

Chris then entered the financial services and advisory industry and during his 16 years of high-level experience he managed over 30 million dollars in assets, specializing in alternative investments, retirement strategies, and wealth accumulation.

Using his expert knowledge in finance, he has successfully bought, renovated and sold hundreds of properties in WNY. With a passionate belief that success in real estate is NOT determined by your actual resources, it's determined by how resourceful you can be. Chris speaks to thousands about how money works and how to place your money in motion to generate a return for you. You must understand that money has always been and will always be the most important tool you will ever use to build the life you want.

Through his success in real estate, Chris and his wife own seven companies, founded Flipout Academy which is a results-based education system that focuses on students' success. They hold over $8,000,000 in real estate and had their own TV show *Risky Builders* air on HGTV along with a few of their renovations featured on other HGTV shows.

9

Mark Schultz

Turnaround Specialist

"For the strength of the Pack is the Wolf, and the strength of the Wolf is the Pack." Rudyard Kipling

SPECIALTIES: Board of Directors, Chief Executive Officer\President, Chief Operating Officer, Vice President Operations, Supply Chain, & Logistics, Strategic Planning & Tactical Execution, Manufacturing & Operational Efficiencies, Profit & Loss, Budget Planning, Supply Chain Management & Sourcing Optimization, 3PL, Contract Manufacturing, Global Multi-site Operations, Cross Functional Team Development

▶ Instilled discipline, process improvement, and cultural change for a Native American Tribe resulting in reduced costs for $55 million balanced budget and over $1million yearly surplus.

▶ Secured largest contract in a company's history, over $100 million, multi-year government contract.

▶ Supported over 100%, 4-year sales growth, and 300% growth in profit at Sierra Concrete Design, Inc. successfully positioning company for private equity funding by streamlining supply and manufacturing operations, instituted best practices, and increased production capacity.

▶ Fostered and supported over 30% increase in sales over two years for NiteRider Technical Lighting during recessionary times through lean operational and logistics efficiencies.

▶ Led squadron recognized two years in a row as the "Best in Class" division in the region, and by the Secretary of Defense among over 500 facilities, as one of the most efficient/innovative aviation maintenance & logistics operations in the Armed Services.

Mark Schultz

▶ 760-936-7253 ▶ MGSchultz7@cox.net ▶
http://www.linkedin.com/in/markschultz

R. Michael Buehler

CEO/Founder at
ACTS Freedom Farms of America

"Leadership is solving problems the day soldiers have stopped giving you problems is the day you have stopped leading them." Colin Powell

I have dedicated more than 30 years to the introduction and education of "Cause Related Marketed Marketing." These last 3 years has focused on ACTS Freedom Farms of America and this program will deliver the greatest "Cause Related Marketing" program ever developed. www.ACTSFFA.com

ACTS has launched Freedom Farm locations in the first few locations and we anticipate the delivery of fresh, nutritional, great tasting produce to those local markets late in the 4th quarter of 2018. In addition to the food values delivered, ACTS Freedom Farms has a plan to establish 112 locations around the US within the next 5-years, while creating more than 50,000 new jobs for Americans with a special focus on America's heroes...our Veterans.

Specialties: Work with public servants, churches, charities, and business owners to create strategic relationships to benefit all parties involved. Public Speaking on self-development, Cause Marketing, Uniting Commerce & Compassion, Personal Spiritual growth, & "Cooperation VS Competition".

What one book do you feel are amustthat you highly recommend others to read? The Bible focusing on the book of Acts.

What movie touched you by its meaning or inspired you? Ferris Bueller's Day Off – it made me famous overnight!

What discipline could someone learn from you? Patience

When "winning someone over" do you think facts or emotions carry the day? Emotions...when dealing with the mind there are too many interruptions due to reasoning (spontaneous excuses). When dealing with the heart, it is more likely to discover the truth.

What will you do differently this year from last year or what do you want more of? Physical exercise to build my body back up after surviving cancer. Four years ago, I decided I needed to lose weight...to date I have lost 150#!

In helping others, is it better to teach them, give them, or show them? Teach them...empowering permanent change.

Why did you start your business? To share the Good News. When Jesus walked the earth, and performed miracles, he never asked if someone qualified. Yet the common dominator in all the stories is that they would ask "why did you do this" because they felt unworthy. And His response was "because my Father sent me."

R. Michael Buehler Buhehler, Sr. aka *"Mr. Cause Marketing"*

"Merging Commerce and Compassion to Utilize the **World's** Money

for God's Purpose"

♛ Cause Marketing Expert ♛ Self-Development Public Speaking
♛ Personal Spiritual Growth ♛

♟ rmb@acts.ws ♟ www.actsffa.com ♟ www.acts.ws

Jeffrey Duff

**CFO ▪ Vocational Education
Veteran Advocate ▪ Speaker
Humanitarian**

"With the possible exception of the equator, everything begins somewhere."
--- C. S. Lewis

Ice Hockey from age 4 into my high school years instilled toughness. The College journey instilled drive and reason. Losing my brother in my early 20's brought humility and faith. Wildland fire fighting with the BLM showed me the power of nature. The wind energy industry fueled the entrepreneur spirit, which has been growing for the last sixteen years.

Today, I am proud to have a role in guiding a nationally successful and fast-growing vocational training company helping to execute the DoD Skillbridge program on active duty military bases around the country and focused on transitioning service members. Along with our Tehachapi CA campus focused on veterans, we have trained over 4500 students and growing and helped partner them with veteran ready companies in high growth industries to launch their civilian careers.

▶ Helped start, build and grow a national vocational training program focused on helping over 4000 veterans find a career to execute their civilian mission of life.

▶ Worked in the early ever-changing wind industry to help shape the direction of performance analysis.

▶ Successfully navigated the growth of a training sector through a new U.S. Department of Defense transition process into one of the most successful military transition solutions of modern time.

Specialties: C-Level Financial Planning/ Corporate Risk Management / Training and Facilitating / Public Speaking / Corporate Facilitator

jeffduff@air-streams.com 661-822-5624 www.air-streams.com

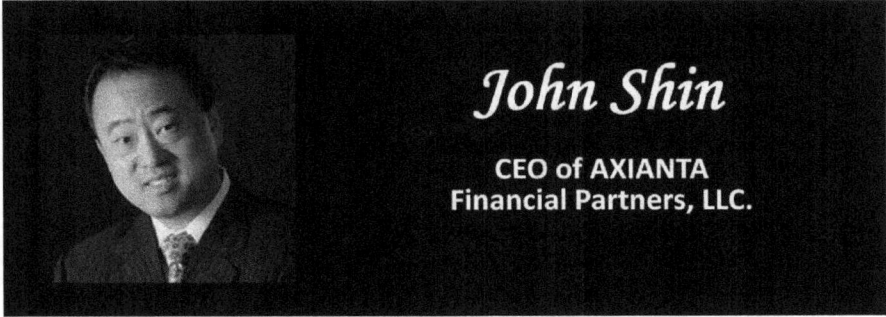

John Shin
CEO of AXIANTA Financial Partners, LLC.

John Shin is the Founder and CEO of AXIANTA Financial Partners, LLC. (AFP) and has created his own progressive sales and personal growth training company made up of professional mentors and business builders who work one-on-one with individuals, businesses and major corporations to help them achieve growth in any economy.

He is also the Founder of a non-profit organization called "ALL FOR ONE" which provides child prosperity centers for children around the world. he has empowered people to achieve peak performance in business, sales, money, teams, relationships and life.

He has mentored and trained, not hundreds, but thousands of people around the country to become successful business owners. His greatest joy is to teach and train businesses grow and achieve true success.

www.ingramcontent.com/pod-product-compliance
Lightning Source LLC
Chambersburg PA
CBHW062218270326
41930CB00009B/1785